AF715144

Save Money Now
Second Edition

TABLE OF CONTENTS

1. BACKGROUND 1
   1.1 INTRODUCTION 1
   1.2 WHAT HAPPENED NEXT 2
   1.3 TAKE ACTION 3
2. KNOW THY ENEMIES 5
   2.1 INTRODUCTION 5
   2.2 CHANGE OF ATTITUDE 5
   2.3 MARKETING TRICKS 9
   2.4 KNOWLEDGE IS POWER 12
3. THE BUDGET PLAN 16
   3.1 INTRODUCTION 16
   3.2 TRACK EXPENSES 17
   3.3 IDENTIFY INITIAL SAVINGS 18
   3.4 PREPARE ANNUAL BUDGET 18
   3.5 TRACK DAILY EXPENSES 19
   3.6 ACTUAL EXPENSES VERSUS BUDGET 19
   3.7 IDENTIFY FURTHER SAVINGS 19
   3.8 STICKING TO THE BUDGET 20
4. GET ORGANISED 25
   4.1 INTRODUCTION 25
   4.2 THE PLAN 26
   4.3 STAY DECLUTTERED 28
   4.4 BECOME SUPER ORGANISED 32
   4.5 CLEANING SCHEDULE 35
5. CUTTING COSTS 37
   5.1 INTRODUCTION 37
   5.2 ACCOMMODATION 38
   5.3 GROCERY SHOPPING 43
   5.4 UTILITIES 68
   5.5 TRANSPORT 84
   5.6 COMMUNICATION 91
   5.7 CLOTHES 93
   5.8 ENTERTAINMENT 99
   5.9 EDUCATION 114
   5.10 FINANCIAL SERVICES 117
   5.11 HEALTH 124

5.12 HOME ITEMS 129
5.13 CHILDREN 133
6. FRUGAL MEALS 137
7. DISASTER PLAN 145
7.1 INTRODUCTION 145
7.2 PRE-PLANNING 146
7.3 REDUNDANCY 149
8. MAKING MONEY 154
9. USEFUL WEBSITES 159
10. ESSENTIAL READING & VIDEOS 161
10.1 BOOKS 161
10.2 YOUTUBE VIDEOS 162

1. BACKGROUND

"We make ourselves rich by making our wants few." - Henry David Thoreau

1.1 Introduction

There is an old saying that "when the US economy sneezes, the rest of the world catches a cold." Well, those days are long gone as the situation has rapidly progressed from a single sneeze to a case of life-threatening influenza in a hospital intensive care unit.

With economic troubles in the USA, Europe and Asia morphing into a global recession (or worse), now is the time to start making preparations for a long, cold winter of tough times. Quite simply, the wild party of easy credit is over. The hangover will be ugly and the sober new world of finance will require a frugal attitude towards money. Chaotic conditions in all types of markets will cause havoc with ordinary people's savings and investments. Gone will be the days of NINJA (no income, no job and no assets) loans and multiple credit card offers. People will have to learn to live within their means and that is going to be very, very hard after such a long period of reckless spending.

Over the last 40 odd years, the world as we knew it was based on endless consumerism. It was normal to hear television advertisements singing the song of 'buy now, pay later'. Credit cards were maxed out to the limit and many people went completely overboard with their spending. Society created the illusion that good times were here to stay indefinitely. Ironically, this was exactly how people felt in the 1920's – just before the Great Depression hit early in the following decade.

Unfortunately, you can put off paying back debts for only so long. Eventually, the piper has to be paid. The global debt situation as it stands now is unsustainable and just like major cracks in the foundation of a house, eventually it **will** collapse. How that fallout will happen has many economists scratching their heads, but there is one sure bet – it won't be pretty and it won't be orderly either.

1.2 What Happened Next

Central banks around the world are as clueless (and impotent) as each other. Smaller countries have little choice but to hang on for the ride and follow the lead of the larger economies. In 2008, the USA Federal Reserve chose the wrong fork in the road after the collapse of Lehman Brothers, a relatively large investment bank. That was the point where fatal decisions were made and banks became 'too big to fail'. By nationalising their debts and putting them onto the public purse string, their economic fate was sealed. Debts of billions turned into trillions and with an ageing population and massive social security commitments (plus a few wars), the ability to repay this astronomical, exponentially-increasing debt became physically impossible. Right on cue, out came the printing presses or quantitative easing (QE) as it became known in the media. QEI was followed by QEII in rapid succession. In December 2012 with a fiscal cliff approaching, QEIII became an uncapped amount and effectively limitless. They were just kicking the can down the road...

Up to that point, if people weren't becoming scared, they should have been. History clearly shows that printing money has never worked to solve a country's economic problems. It just delays the inevitable and makes what would have been a bad situation turn into something much, much worse. Printing money ultimately leads to inflation. It's just a question of how soon things get to a point where ordinary people can no longer pay for things. Hungry stomachs often lead to civil unrest and history shows a clear path – boom, bust, depression, war.

Every country in the world operates in the global economy to varying degrees. This means that major trouble in developed or first world countries will have a domino effect on all economies. Ultimately, there will be <u>no</u> place to hide to avoid the fallout of higher unemployment and crime rates. However, regardless of whether your job is a safe port in a rough sea or you can see the firing squad loading their rifles, there are steps you can follow to prepare for tough economic times.

1.3 Take Action

A lot of people are very worried. They are seeing obvious signs around their neighbourhood that all is not well. Newspapers scream out headlines of major businesses that have collapsed and hundreds of staff being made redundant. Stock market indices rise and fall with gut-wrenching swings as confidence levels take on a schizophrenic madness. Listings for both commercial and residential real estate have sky-rocketed and many advertisements are for mortgagee sales. Unsold homes sit on the market for months or even years and only sell after a significant price reduction. Crime levels are increasing and civil unrest demonstrations in places like Greece regularly make front page news.

Being very worried for a sustained period of time is not going to do your health any good. One of the greatest cures for worry is action and taking steps to alleviate the problem. Being prepared for the worst, but hoping for the best is a sensible plan. Educating yourself as to exactly what is going on in the world economy is also important.

Start your education by performing an internet search on key luminaries such as: Jim Rogers, Marc Faber, Steve Keen, Jim Rickards, Peter Schiff, Nuriel Rubini, George Soros and Gerald Celente. David Walker, the former US Comptroller General (the nation's top accountant) is one of the best qualified speakers on the USA economy. Sadly, not enough people are listening. Free newsletters such as the Daily Reckoning (www.dailyreckoning.com) can add further to your understanding of the serious economic problems the world is facing.

Building on this internet-inspired education, is this book. It was born from frustration at going to hundreds of different websites searching for tips and hints to become more frugal and save money. It aims to put everything into the one book and deliver a clear, simple guide on how to be better prepared for the hard-economic times ahead. Even if things don't get as bad as predicted, it can't hurt to be prepared and ultimately save money in the process.

Living a life that is free from the clutter of mindless materialism is a new kind of freedom. People are hungry for a different way of living which reduces their debt levels and allows them more time with friends and family. Being frugal is not the same as being a cheapskate or tightwad with money. Instead, it's being careful, cautious and conservative with every function of daily living. In the end, if the fertiliser does hit the fan for the global economy, after reading this book you will be in a much better position to duck and cover from the worst of it.

2. KNOW THY ENEMIES

"Attitude is a little thing that makes a big difference." - Winston Churchill

2.1 Introduction

Part of the battle towards financial freedom involves knowing the enemy, of which there are two and both are equally powerful and both work together. One enemy lurks within your subconscious urging you to buy things. It's entwined with your self-esteem and has one eye firmly planted on the famous Jones family. Keeping up with the Jones' is an internal mantra which almost everyone carries with them to some degree. If you can master this enemy, you are well on your way to financial freedom.

The other enemy is the full force of the marketing industry who has studied human psychology to the point where they know you better than you know yourself. Everything they do is designed to pull at the wallet strings and separate you from your money. If you want to be successful and survive in tough times, you need to understand and master both enemies.

2.2 Change of Attitude

In this consumer-focussed world, everything around you is telling you the ideal way to live. From the moment you wake, there is someone out there trying to sell you something. It might be the morning newspaper or internet banner advertising. It might be the massive billboards at the train station. It could also be the t-shirt worn by the person standing in front of you in a bus queue. However, it is achieved, the world we live in is all about selling you the idea that you **need** things.

In evolutionary theory, there are the concepts of 'natural selection' and 'survival of the fittest'. Although they have different meanings and biologists prefer the term 'natural selection', the overriding message is that if a living organism is going to have even half a chance at surviving, they cannot be weak. These tough times ahead will also create economic winners and losers. To increase your chances of survival, you need to change your attitude. It is your first and last line of defence against the relentless push to spend money. Every dollar needs to be stretched further and that's really hard when inflation is causing everything to get more and more expensive. Many people walk around with certain types of messages circulating in their brains. These phrases fall into one of two categories:

Procrastination

- Things will sort themselves out in the end.
- I need to marry someone rich so I won't have money problems.
- I'll sort out a budget next week, next term, next year etc.
- After I've finished school, college etc. then I'll sort out a budget.
- It's just too hard to keep track of my money.

Justification

- It's easier for them. They have family to help them out.
- If they have a new (television / computer / car etc.) then we must get one too.
- It's okay to buy this because it is on sale.
- Everyone else has got one.
- I deserve it. I've earned it.
- I won't spend so much, next time.
- It's Christmas for goodness sake!
- Just this once.

Procrastination and justification both need to be banished to get ahead financially. These wretched messages need to be re-programmed and a new, frugal set of rules needs to be followed before any money is handed over to buy things.

If you like that gut-wrenching feeling of not having enough money to pay the rent or some other essential bill, then read no further. However, for most of us the thought of being poor is very, very stressful. Poverty and poor health have a strong track record of co-existing. With increased rates of substance abuse and high divorce rates that follow, it can be a downward spiral that is extremely difficult to escape. Yet with lots of initiative, creativity and strength it is possible to break the cycle – although far better to avoid the situation in the first place.

Having financial problems is a lot like being caught in a rip current at sea. Firstly, it can happen to anyone regardless of their occupation or debt levels. Rips also don't discriminate based on age, sex, race or religion. They don't look at your bank account either before sucking you far out into the ocean. However, what matters most in this deadly situation is your **attitude**. Are you going to act rationally and go with the flow until it's safe to swim sideways to the rip and escape? Or are you going to commission a full-scale panic attack and fight the unwinnable by swimming against the rip, thereby dramatically increasing your chances of drowning?

To prepare for a financial crisis, you need to take responsibility for yourself. For certain, there will be friends, family or even entire governments that you can blame for letting you down in the past. Nobody has a perfect life or perfect parents or even a perfect government running their country. In fact, most people have politicians more focussed on being re-elected than actually doing the job they were paid to do.

If the past or the present was filled with hardship, focus on the future and putting things right. Throw a symbolic pebble over your shoulder and don't look back. Move forward with your life and make changes now to improve the situation. Count your blessings and remember that there is no such thing as a free lunch. Nothing truly worth achieving is easy. Here are seven tips to help change your attitude to money:

- **Repeat affirmations**: Working in a similar manner to prayer, affirmations can help your subconscious work on solutions to fix your current financial situation. At least once a day, ideally before going to bed, repeat a mantra of positive affirmations about money. Some suggestions are things like:
  - I will always earn more money than I spend.
  - Each day, I will work on finding new ways to save money.
  - Money will come into my life and I will resist spending it.
  - Money gives me more choices in my life.

- **Visualise your future self:** Your sub-conscious is far more powerful than you can ever imagine. Take the time each day to picture your future exactly the way you would like it to be. The clearer the picture, the clearer the goals become and the faster your brain can work out a solution to achieving them.

- **Positive social interactions:** There is an old saying that 'birds of a feather, flock together'. If you have friends and family that spend their time complaining about everything but doing nothing about it, then you need to move on. Find people who are intent on improving their situation and their positive energy (and ideas) will flow on to you.

- **Self-education:** Learn about money and investing by reading magazines and books from the library or by reading articles on the internet. Sadly, the concept of money management has been left out of the education system which means <u>you</u> have to take the initiative and fill the gap yourself.

- **Play Monopoly or chess:** Board games are a great way to train your brain to think. Play Monopoly with gusto until you learn the importance of saving to buy things (property) and techniques to build on your wealth once you've acquired it. Crossword puzzles are also good exercise for hazy brains that have grown cobwebs.

- **Treat money with respect:** Money is important. Fold notes carefully in your wallet and keep track of loose change. Put any spare coins into a money box rather than have them burn a hole in your pocket. Always pick up coins you drop or find on the ground – no matter how small. Remember that you usually have to earn around $1.30 to keep $1.00 because of taxation.

- **Get back to nature:** Nothing shakes off the shackles of modern society as fast as a weekend camping. Ideally this is in an area without showers or modern toilets. Living without basic facilities helps you realise that there are so many things we take for granted in western society and many of them are not *needs* but *wants*.

2.3 Marketing Tricks

The marketing industry's main goal is to get you to buy things. They will stop at nothing in their ruthless battle for your hard-earned dollars. To counteract this assault, you need to understand that businesses are not charities. They are solely out to make money and if an offer seems too good to be true, then it best to walk away from the deal. There will *always* be another opportunity – despite what they might tell you. Here are some of the tricks they use:

- **Prices ending in 99 cents**: In psychological studies it's been shown that people are more likely to buy something that is priced at $9.99 rather than $10.00.

- **Buy one get one free**: Do you seriously think the retailer is selling these products at a loss? It just goes to show you what a considerable mark up these companies place on just one item – let alone two of them! Stop and think before buying. If you never really needed *one* item in the first place, why on earth are you buying *two*?

- **Suggestive selling:** Nowhere does this work better than at McDonalds and their "Would you like fries with your order?" It certainly works as many people that only came in for a drink or a burger find themselves walking out with additional items they never intended to buy.

- **Hurry now, limited offer**: Why are they in such a rush? Quite simply, they want your money in a hurry. You need to think the opposite and slow down. Take your time. There really is no good reason for you to rush, hurry, stampede etc. In fact, the more time you take deciding to buy something, the greater the chances you'll stop and realise you don't need it. This is exactly why they want you to hurry; because they don't want you to go cold on the sale. Remember that time kills all deals.

- **In store bakery:** Nothing tempts people more than the smell of freshly baked bread. Many supermarkets have an in-store bakery just for this purpose. Even the slightest aroma of fresh bread gets people hungry and they end up buying far more food than they intended.

- **Soft lighting:** Look up to the ceiling next time you are in the fruit and vegetable section of a grocery store. Inevitably it will be soft lighting to hide any flaws in the produce.

- **Clever placements**: The most common items on everyone's shopping list are bread and milk. So naturally you would expect they should be located close to each other and in an easily accessible location. Wrong. Supermarkets want to keep you inside their store for as long as possible and so they are usually located at the far end of the store and widely separated from each other.

- **Follow the trail**: Studies have shown that in the USA, people like to do their grocery shopping in a counter-clockwise direction. For this reason, stores try to put the door on the right-hand side of the building (or at least force you in some way to start shopping in this direction.) Then they place their best produce (usually fresh fruit and vegetables) right in your migratory path. Their goal is to set the scene for your shopping experience by creating the impression that everything is **fresh**. In Australia, UK and other countries that drive on the left-hand side of the road, people tend to follow a clockwise direction – if the store allows them to do it. Either way, management know that people are like sheep and tend to walk around a store the same way each time they visit. You need to understand that every part of a shop is planned out in a way to trigger as much impulse spending as possible.

- **Removing currency symbols**: It has been shown in market research that menu items that are missing currency symbols such as $ or £ lead to increased sales. Dollar signs remind people of the money being paid!

- **Quote daily costs**: It sounds so much cheaper to say that things like gym memberships cost only $3.00 per day rather than $1095 per year. Insurance and mobile phone companies are well known for using this technique to trick customers into signing up for their products.

- **Loss leaders**: McDonalds is the master of marketing and nowhere is this more apparent than their soft serve ice-cream cones that sell in Australia for $0.30. It's the cheapest ice-cream on the market and it draws in crowds of parents and their children. Once people are in the store, it just becomes all too easy to get fries or a burger and drinks.

- **SALE signs**: In these tough times, many retailers are getting desperate. Gone are the days of 20% off sales. Instead many shops are advertising 60 - 80% cuts or higher! These types of sales have become ubiquitous particularly for fashion stores where clothes are perpetually on sale.

- **Manipulative use of colour**: It's no mistake that fast food restaurants are covered in bright red, orange and yellow. These colours are known to stimulate the appetite and also be attractive to children and adults alike. Blue is seen as a more trustworthy colour which is why it's used for medication and is a common colour scheme for financial institutions. However, light purple is apparently the colour that is most likely to make people spend money!

- **Mood music**: It's hard not to notice the loud top 10 music blaring from clothes shops that are aiming to attract the teenage market. Grocery stores use a similar technique by playing light, uplifting, easy-listening songs that fit the age group of the average middle-aged shopper. At Christmas, listen for the sound of 'Jingle Bells' where shops are hoping to jingle some money out of your wallet and set you in the mood for a holiday spending spree.

- **Bling**: Humans are like bower birds and are attracted to bright, shiny surfaces such as mirrors and sparkling lights. It should be no surprise then that shopping malls have shiny, tiled floors and bright, twinkling lights.

- **Gift cards:** The lure of a gift card or voucher promising 20% off your next purchase can be hard to resist. One of the best strategies is to re-gift the gift and make someone else happy from your overwhelming generosity.

- **Free trials**: This is where you sign up for something you like for a free three-month trial period. Then after the three months, you've completely forgotten that it's no longer free and the bills start rolling in. Be very wary about signing up for anything free if it involves handing over your credit card details.

- **Repetitive television advertisements:** These are the clever little jingles that you can't get out of your head. Suddenly before you know it that cleverly advertised brand is sitting in your trolley and being scanned by the checkout operator.

- **Infomercials:** Women at home with babies and young children are the prime target as they often turn to daytime television as a diversion. Infomercials almost always involve an audience of other women cheering on a product and acting as if it's the best thing since sliced bread. Lots of clapping, smiling, laughing and approving nods. Women with young children are typically sleep deprived and tired people often make poor money decisions.

- **Lots of words**: Think about whether you would order 'baked fish' or 'cod marinated in butter sauce' from a restaurant menu. People often interpret more words as better value.

2.4 Knowledge is Power

"When the student is ready, the master appears." Buddhist Proverb

It is human nature to take the easiest path in life and become addicted to instant gratification. It's also a remnant from childhood where toddlers demand things they want **NOW**! Without guidance and support, children grow into adults with limited patience and self-discipline. Add in additional pressure from a very clever and manipulative advertising industry and society ends up brainwashed to believe that something they *want* is really a *need*. Social pressure from friends and family then go on to finish off the job.

2.4.1 Being Frugal

Understanding both the internal and external pressures everyone faces is the *first* step in the journey towards becoming smarter with money and surviving tough economic times. These pressures are relentless and extremely powerful forces. Yet it is possible to overcome them and win the war against the process of extracting money from your wallet.

Being frugal doesn't mean having to give up every single luxury in life and live in a perpetual state of denial. Instead the goal is to extract maximum value from every dollar you spend and minimise waste on everything else. The end result is that you can build an emergency fund of savings for unexpected events and are prepared for whatever life throws at you. Stress levels reduce quickly when you have a backup plan at the ready with a healthy emergency fund of money.

Learn off the magical equation below and understand that if you can maximise your INCOME and minimise your EXPENSES then you will have larger SAVINGS. Being frugal helps you minimise your expenses. In tough times it gets even harder to maximise your income particularly when there are fewer jobs on offer. Chapter 8 covers off ideas to improve the income side of the equation. The rest of this book focusses on helping you reduce your expenses. The overall goal is to get you into a position where you have savings squirrelled away in an emergency savings account and can sleep soundly at night.

2.4.2 Learning the Ropes

It's important to distinguish the term 'frugal' from 'cheapskate'. A cheapskate is a stingy person who is so tight with their money they go to extremes to achieve their goals. They are unlikely to ever give to charity and often use (and abuse) other people's goodwill. Cheapskates or tightwads such as Ebenezer Scrooge in Charles Dickens' novel 'A Christmas Carol' are at the extreme end of the spectrum. They often end up in an even worse situation because they lose friendships that could potentially help them out in tough times. In contrast, frugal people are often generous with their time and goodwill. They are more concerned with getting good value for their money and are willing to pay more for quality goods and services.

Don't be tempted to head down the path of extreme behaviour. Find a middle ground and be prepared to help others along the way. Granted that it's not possible to help everyone, but have a rule where you make a conscious effort to help *someone* in some way, every day. Altruism is a great way of counteracting depression and building a high self-esteem.

Everyone faces tough times at some point in their lives but it's often through adversity that we learn our greatest lessons. The grass may seem greener on the other side but that green eye of jealous often becomes blind to all the efforts required to keep the grass looking so good.

Being frugal is a lifestyle choice and it is best described by the quote, 'Use it up, wear it out, and make it do or do without.' Many people have a frugal lifestyle thrust upon them by circumstances that are beyond their control. Economic recessions have a nasty habit of taking down good people and throwing their finances into a high-speed blender.

Yet many of the richest people in the world choose to lead a highly frugal lifestyle. For example, Britain's Queen Elizabeth II is renowned for turning off lights and heating to save costs. Over in the USA, Warren Buffet a famous, wealthy investor, still lives in the home he bought in 1958 for $31,500.

Regardless of circumstances, people need to learn to live within (or below) their means and stop the cycle of instant gratification. It's a tough ask when society puts everyone under so much pressure to conform to a consumer-led lifestyle. But the alternative is bankruptcy, divorce, poor health, high stress levels and debt collectors knocking at the door. It's always a better outcome if you make the decision to jump before you are pushed. Tackle financial problems front on and remember that recessions don't last forever. At the end of the day, family and friends are more important than owning lots of stuff.

2.4.3 How to say 'No'

Inevitably you will be asked to buy things for school fundraising or charity events. This is a deeply personal decision but one that you need to address in your budget before people solicit you for money. A good tactic is to decide on one or two charities that you will support each year. Decline other requests with grace by using the 'hug and release' technique. Say something like, "I understand this charity is important to you but my family donates to two other charities and we don't have funds for anything more." Another quick alternative is the very simple, "No thank-you."

School and church charity fundraising events can often be much harder to decline as you often know the person asking you for money. For these circumstances, it's best to come up with a counter-offer by asking if there is another way you can help. Perhaps that is through helping set up stalls for the fete or doing gardening around the church yard.

3. THE BUDGET PLAN

"A budget is telling your money where to go instead of wondering where it went." *Dave Ramsey*

3.1 Introduction

Setting up a budget may seem to be the most boring task on the planet. Many people probably think it has the same excitement level as completing their annual tax return. However, in tough times people need to get past preconceived notions and face the facts. Whether it's boring or not, if you are spending more than you earn, then you are heading for big trouble.

Most people have difficulty putting together a budget plan because they only ever do one part of it. The vast majority of books and websites teach people to create a list of all their expenses and sources of income. If the estimated incoming funds are greater than the estimated outgoing funds, then all is well. The trouble is that those estimates are **not** reality!

A key part of an effective budget plan is to track <u>both</u> expenses and income. This means recording all income and expense items <u>every</u> single day. After getting into the habit of tracking, you can then start analysing where the money is going and search for ways to reduce spending. It needs to be a continuous improvement process with monthly reviews on how things are going.

There is simply no point having a budget if you fail to track your actual expenses. It's just a huge waste of time. Everything is just a guess and that means you never really know how much you are spending (or saving)!

3.2 Track Expenses

Before you even think about putting together an annual budget, you need to track each and every expense for at least one month. That means, every time you hand over money for ***anything***, you have to make a record in either a MS-Excel spread sheet or notebook. Tracking expenses will force you to think about money and focus on your goals.

Don't forget simple items like a daily coffee or soft drink from a vending machine. All these little items end up becoming a much larger cost when you add them up over the course of a year. It's an absolute guarantee that the first month of tracking will be the biggest financial eye-opener of your entire life!

Surprisingly, it doesn't take a lot of time to track expenses. In fact, it should only ever take about five minutes each day. If it's taking longer than this, then you either have all your bills due on the one day or (more likely) have a serious spending problem. That's why it's so important to track your spending. It helps identify where you are falling down in your budget.

It's very, very easy to track expenses. Just ask for a receipt whenever you hand over money. If that's not possible, then write the amount in a notebook that you carry with your purse or wallet. Remember to also check bank statements to ensure you haven't forgotten any automatic payments. An example of a typical expense list is shown below.

Date	Item Description	Amount (AUD)
02/01/2019	Morning coffee with friends	$ 4.50
02/01/2019	Petrol for car (weekly)	$ 62.50
02/01/2019	Clothes shopping	$ 88.99
04/01/2019	Lunch from cafeteria	$ 9.80
04/01/2019	Rent (weekly)	$ 250.00

3.3 Identify Initial Savings

Once you have tracked all your expenses for one month, it's time to start analysing where the money is going and work out where you can make initial cutbacks. One of the most obvious places to save money involves **food**. The morning coffee with friends and lunch from the work cafeteria are not essential expenses. Instead they are an example of discretionary spending. If you are serious about cutting your budget, items like this need to be banished.

Think carefully. It's not going to kill you to prepare lunch at home and take it to work. Plus, many workplaces have a kitchen or at least a fridge. Similarly, you don't really need to drink coffee at work when there are other alternatives. A lot of people are wasting at least $5.00 - $10.00 (AUD) a day for unnecessary food items. These can easily add up to at least $1826 (AUD) or more each year. Ouch!

3.4 Prepare Annual Budget

After you have analysed your spending for one month and identified areas where you can cut back, it's time to put together an annual budget. Either create your own or find a free template at www.vertex42.com.

Start identifying expenses by using old bank statements and receipts. Going through your address list will also trigger your memory for annual expenses such as: insurance, magazine subscriptions and school books etc. Don't expect to get your annual budget one hundred per cent correct the first time you do it. Instead, make adjustments throughout the first year for essential items that you've forgotten. It's the second year of budgeting that will prove to be far more accurate and refined.

Remember to include provision for any taxes that are due during your budget period. This is just the kind of item that can throw a cat amongst the pigeons and send everyone into a flying panic. Also, remember to account for inflation so if for example your car insurance was $500.00 last year, make sure you estimate around $525.00 for the next year's budget. Alternatively, ring your insurance company and get a quote for the following year.

3.5 Track Daily Expenses

This step is basically the same as the expense tracking you did initially for one month. However, this time you're actually tracking the expenses against what you have budgeted. Your goal is to ensure that LESS money is leaving your bank account than what's coming INTO your bank account. It's now that you are actively striving to meet your estimated budget target and cut spending.

3.6 Actual Expenses versus Budget

This is the moment of truth in the entire budgeting process. Have you kept to the plan? Have you finished the month either breaking even or ideally with a surplus? If not, then it's a cause for reflection on why you haven't met your goal.

There should never be any surprises at the end of the month unless there's been some sort of accident or crisis. Let's face it though, bad things do happen, which is why you need to have an 'Emergency Fund' setup as quickly as possible. You need to make the sacrifices now so that you have something set aside in case of disaster. Once you have some rainy-day savings set aside, then small luxuries can be re-introduced.

3.7 Identify Further Savings

Nothing worth achieving has ever been easy. Expect to feel some initial pain from the whole process. However, the rewards will be far, far greater than any minor inconveniences you may encounter on your journey to achieving a budget surplus!

Chapter 5 of this book outlines detailed cost cutting ideas for your budget. It's a simple matter of reading through them all and working out which ones you can incorporate into your lifestyle.

3.8 Sticking to the Budget

Follow these 22 handy tips to stick to your budget:

- **Have a goal:** It's great to have a budget and know exactly where your money is being spent, but if you don't have an end goal in mind it will be far too easy to abandon the plan. Make sure you set a specific savings target. Whether that goal is saving 10% of your income or saving a specific amount like $10,000 to hold in an emergency fund - the goal needs to be quantifiable.

- **Pay essential bills first:** This tip goes against the grain when it comes to lots of other advice out there on the internet. Typical budget advice says to *always* pay yourself first. Obviously, this advice comes from people who have never received an electricity, gas, phone, water, insurance and massive dental bill all in the one month! You simply have to pay the essential bills first, and then pay yourself by putting money aside into an emergency cash account that's for - drum roll - emergencies!

- **Only carry cash:** Keep your credit card at home and only use it for items where you would need to carry ridiculous amounts of cash making it a safety risk. However, always carry a small amount of cash for emergencies.

- **Shop alone:** Never do the food shopping as a couple as each person will inevitably have a different idea of what to load into the trolley. Don't even think of taking children with you!

- **Set up an emergency fund:** Emergency money is not for discretionary spending on things like holidays, concert tickets, parties etc. Emergencies are for things like urgent dental work, medical bills, unexpected redundancy etc. Your goal should be to have enough money in your emergency fund to keep your household running for at least six months.

  Now, that's a LOT of money and it will take you time to accumulate it. But the feeling of freedom and reduced stress that you will experience will be worth all the sacrifices you'll need to make to get yourself into this position. In the olden days, they called it 'saving for a rainy day' where people couldn't work (and get paid), if the weather was bad. If possible, arrange to have 10% of your salary transferred directly from your main bank account into a special, high-interest bank account each payday. This way, it's locked up before you get a chance to spend it.

- **Know a *need* from a *want*:** This seems to be one of the hardest lessons to learn in life and one that most people struggle to comprehend. A need is something like: shelter (home), food, clothing or medical services. A want is something like: tickets to a concert, fashionable clothes, holidays or buying a flash car. You need to sort out the differences and make sure you have money for the necessities in life and for your emergency fund. Once you have things organised, then you can start thinking about indulging in a few small luxuries.

- **Keep away from shopping malls:** Remember that shopping centres are designed specifically to get you to spend money. The longer you are inside a shop, the more likely you are to spend. Avoid temptation and don't set foot in them.

- **Outsmart temptation:** When you head into the grocery store, make sure you have four things - a shopping list, electronic calculator to keep track of the total bill, **cash only** and a full stomach.

- **Shop online:** Not only will you get a better bargain because the online retailer doesn't have to pay expensive landlord costs, but you also get the chance to stop and think before you buy. There is also a much greater range of designs and products. However, just remember to include shipping costs and insurance in all your calculations!

- **Pay down debt:** If you have a credit card debt, then you are likely to be paying the highest rate of interest in the market. Your first priority (before the emergency fund) is to get rid of this debt. The only way to start the process is to cut up the credit card and stop adding to the debt. Once it's chopped into tiny little pieces, you need to focus on paying off the loan immediately.

On the other hand, if you are disciplined with money and can ensure you pay your credit card off in full each month and not incur any interest charges, then a credit card can be your best friend. Simply by understanding the time value of money, it allows you to keep your money in a high interest savings account and pay off the loan up to 55 days later (depending on your credit card terms and conditions). So, you benefit from a free bank loan and collect the interest. The banks allow this to happen only because there are so few people doing it and they are already making a fortune in interest charged on unpaid credit card balances.

- **Avoid direct debits:** There is nothing a business loves more than locking their customers into a monthly direct debit repayment schedule. For many people, they never check their bank statements and never notice the $54.25 being deducted each month. It makes the purchase effectively invisible and that's really, really bad if you are trying to budget! If possible, avoid signing up for anything that involves a company billing you on a monthly basis. It also means you can easily change bank accounts without having to worry about changing automatic payment arrangements.

- **Speak to your bank manager:** Have a chat with your bank manager to ensure you have the most efficient bank account system in place for your circumstances. Remember also that they have sales quotas so don't take everything they say as gospel – they are bank managers not priests! They have a vested interest in getting you to sign up for personal loans, mortgages and high interest credit cards. You need to make sure you sign up for high interest savings accounts and/or term deposits, get yourself out of debt as fast as possible and arrange to pay no fees on any of your transaction accounts. If your bank is uncooperative, tell them you'll take your business elsewhere. If they don't jump to attention, follow through on the threat and move to a bank that truly listens to its customers. If you believe any of their advertising propaganda about "caring for customers", then you truly deserve to part with your hard-earned cash.

- **Get family on board:** You will be fighting a losing battle if you are the only person in the house who is turning off lights and taking a 3-minute shower every night. Not only will it breed resentment but your efforts will be thwarted. Best to get everyone on board and then work out a plan to reward them for their initiative.

- **Collect loose change:** Store spare coins in a jar or piggy bank in the kitchen. It will be a surprise how much extra money you end up saving throughout the year. At Christmas either make a donation to charity or buy a surprise gift for the family.

- **Never buy new what you can buy used:** Items like cars, houses, jewellery, exercise gear, recreational toys, furniture and books immediately lose value the moment they are bought new from a store. Far better to get a good second hand version and save lots of money in the process.

- **Notice any imperfections**: If you notice that the goods you are about to buy are damaged then inform the sales assistant. Don't even think of paying full price for damaged goods. Minor scratches on electrical goods or makeup stains on clothes are imperfections that make the stock item extremely hard for a retailer to sell. It will inevitably end up being scrapped or heavily discounted. Your job is to ask for the 'heavily discounted price' while you are at the store. After all, if you have children, the odds of things getting damaged within about one second of arrival in your home are practically 100%. Slightly damaged goods won't make much difference in the long run except to your bank balance.

- **Be realistic:** Remember that Rome wasn't built in a day and your budgeting skills won't be perfected in a day either. Don't be too hard on yourself if you fall off the wagon and buy something that wasn't planned. When a toddler is learning to walk, they fall over but get right back up again as they perfect the art of walking. It's the same with budgeting and just because you 'fell over' by overspending, it doesn't mean that you will never be successful. Make a note of when and where you've slipped up and take active steps to avoid that same situation again. Knowing yourself is half the battle. Get back on track as quickly as possible and keep striving to meet your budget targets. Try aiming to meet your budget over smaller time periods. So, for example, aim to stick to your budget **today** rather than focusing too heavily on a longer period of time.

- **Allow small rewards:** To ensure your life doesn't turn into a constant battle of denial, it's important to allow for small rewards when you meet your savings targets. This needs to be something that gives maximum enjoyment for minimum cost. For example, going to the movies or buying a cheesecake dessert for dinner. Success should be celebrated but try and make the purchase an experience or memory rather than more stuff to fill the house!

- **Create visual reminders:** It might be a picture of a dream holiday location placed on the fridge or simply a written 'Remember to save money today!' reminder placed inside your wallet.

- **Keep all receipts:** Have a filing system where you scan bank statements, receipts and bills. Alternatively set up accordion folders to store original receipts. Track everything spent in a MS-Excel spread sheet in order to identify your exact financial position.

- **Self-education:** Forget the idea that the education system is going to teach you anything about finance or budgeting. It's rare for any school or college to teach practical money-management skills. However, in the absence of anything else, you need to take responsibility for your own life education by reading books from the library, viewing money saving blogs, attending free seminars and listening to YouTube videos. Remember that self-education shouldn't cost you anything more than your time.

- **Senior or student discounts:** If you are over 50 years old or a student, then remember to ask if there is a discounted price. Often things like travel tickets, restaurant meals and transport can have very attractive rates.

4. GET ORGANISED

"Clutter is nothing more than postponed decisions." *Barbara Hemphill*

The amount of precious time the average person wastes looking for a missing earring, purse, library book or car keys must amount to days or even weeks of their life. It's crazy that people keep repeating the problem again and again while complaining bitterly at the same time. Yet there is another way of running your life so you aren't spinning around in circles looking for lost items. Simple changes can be made to make the general day-to-day routine of a busy life a whole lot easier. However, you have to be prepared to change your mindset – and as we all know, change can be very hard!

4.1 Introduction

Many tip sheets advise people to declutter their homes in stages and attack the problem in small steps starting one room at a time. This is not very effective because it means multiple trips back and forwards to the rubbish tip and charity bins. Inevitably people lose motivation and the end result is that one or two rooms are slightly less cluttered.

No! Go for the big bang approach with a major declutter. Then each week afterwards have smaller decluttering sessions. For items that end up in storage, use the change of season to trigger a review of whether to donate, recycle, keep or throw them out.

The Decluttering Plan

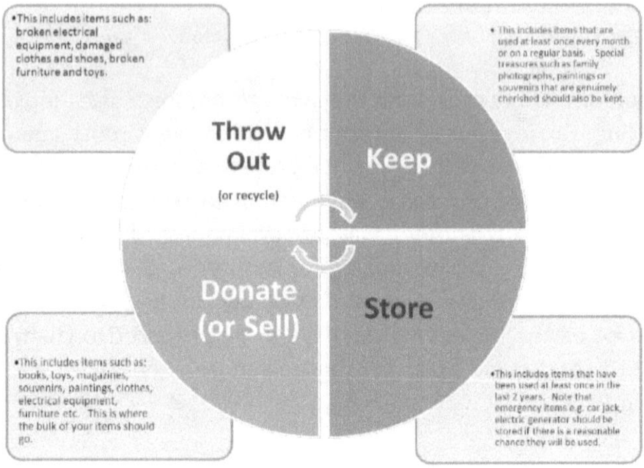

4.2 The Plan

- **Block out a weekend:** Don't try to start this process during the week where everyone is busy rushing to get to work or school. It will be doomed to failure. You need to block out a free weekend and be prepared to roll up your sleeves for the entire time.

- **Tell friends and family:** It's always good to warn the family that a major decluttering event is about to held. It gives them a chance to start focussing on what they want to keep, store, donate, recycle or throw out. It can also give you the opportunity to enlist a team of happy, willing helpers.

- **Prepare the battlefield:** If you anticipate that there will be large items such as furniture (or even old cars) that need to be removed, contact the relevant companies to ensure their services are booked. If you need to hire a mini-skip or trailer, have that ready to arrive on your doorstep mid-morning so you've already had a good few hours to start sorting through items. You will also need large boxes or containers for items you plan to store and sturdy garbage bags for items you plan to donate or throw out.

- **Set the rules:** This will be the hardest part of the process as you establish the rules for decluttering your possessions. The more ruthless you are now, the easier your life will be going forwards. Read the philosophy of simple living at Zenhabits (www.zenhabits.net) where Leo Babauta keeps his possessions to an absolute minimum allowing him to focus more intensely on his goals.

On decluttering day (D-Day), follow these rules to get the maximum results:

1. **KEEP:** This should only be for items that you use on a regular basis. If you have 25 pairs of shoes for example, it's very likely that about 20 of them are not worn on a regular basis. Some of them are obviously going to be too good to throw out so they should be stored in a box with a date label showing when they were last used. If one or two years pass by and they still haven't been used, it's time to move them from the 'Storage' category to the 'Donate' category. If you have trouble working out what to keep, it's a very simple question, "What would I take if I had 10 minutes before a bush fire or flood evacuation?" As a general rule, get rid of any clothing that you haven't worn in 12 months as it's very unlikely you will ever wear it again.

2. **STORE:** Seasonal clothing and any other items that you do not use regularly but still need to use again, should be securely stored to ensure they remain dry and rodent-free. Plastic storage boxes with tight fitting lids should be used as opposed to open cardboard boxes. Items such as camping equipment, skiing gear, gardening tools etc. should be stored in a safe place in your garage.

3. **DONATE (OR SELL):** If items are still in good working order, they should be donated to either friends, charity shops or school fetes. If you are having trouble letting go of an item, take a photo of it so you can keep the memory without the clutter! If you think the item has a market, then arrange to sell it online via EBay, Craigslist or through a garage (or yard) sale.

4. **THROW OUT**: If clothing is damaged or electrical goods do not work, they need to be thrown out. Check your local council for rules on disposing items as not everything can go into a normal recycling or general rubbish bin. Make sure you also clear out your pantry, medicine cabinet and cosmetics supplies as it's very easy to keep things (and even use them) when they have gone way past their expiry date.

4.3 Stay Decluttered

Keeping your home clean and decluttered has obvious benefits for everyone. You will avoid the stress of hunting for lost items and your home will be a lot easier to clean. A simple, clutter-free home is also safer and healthier as you are unlikely to trip over things left lying about. There are also lots of opportunities to save money because you avoid buying unnecessary things and are always up-to-date with bills and other time-dependent activities. Here are 17 tips to help you minimise the clutter in your home:

- **Stay focussed:** Wardrobes, kitchens and laundries are clutter hot spots in every home. If you can keep the clutter to a minimum in these areas, you will be well on your way to an organised home!

- **Be ruthless:** Have a rule that if an item of clutter comes into your house, then something else must be donated or thrown out. Repeat the mantras, 'One in. One out.' If that doesn't work, try these wise words: 'If in doubt, throw it out!'

- **Scan kid's schoolwork:** Rather than keep every item of art or school work that you child has completed, scan their work and bin the rest. It will save a mountain of clutter around the house. Also, create a memory book for each child to hold important certificates and report cards so they are all in the one place and protected from damage.

- **Do not buy books or magazines:** Your local library is the best source of books, magazines and newspapers. These can all be borrowed at zero cost and zero clutter for your home!

- **Buy a set of accordion folders**: Set up a paper filing system for bills, tax records, receipts, warranty items, insurance policies and appliance instructions. Remember that if the original paper copy is not required, that there is even less clutter if you scan the item and just store an electronic version.

- **Remove packaging from food:** As soon as you bring groceries home (or even better do it at the shop), set about removing all the layers of packaging that you possibly can. There is nothing worse than running late in the morning and having to open up containers or run back to the rubbish bin again and again to dispose of plastic wrapping.

- **Re-gift presents:** If you don't like a gift that you have received, make good use of it and re-gift it to someone who will. Just make sure that the original 'giver' never meets up with the new 'receiver'.

- **Train the kids:** Have mantras that you repeat to the kids. For example, when you arrive home say to them, 'Hats in the kitchen. Shoes at the door!' What a surprise, after about 1000 times of saying it, they may actually start doing it! To lighten your load further, assign them age appropriate tasks to help keep the house tidy.

- **Clean as you go:** After using the bathroom, grab some clean toilet paper and quickly wipe over the toilet seat and the areas around it. Roll out a few more sheets of fresh toilet paper and give the hand basin a quick wipe over. Hang up any towels or mats that have found their home on the floor and presto - a bathroom that looks safe to enter! Similarly, never stand around the kitchen waiting for the kettle to boil. Instead use that time to wipe down the bench, fridge and cupboard doors.

- **Clear kitchen bench policy:** Have a rule that the kitchen must have a clear bench tops before going to bed. This means all appliances (except the electric kettle) must be put away along with any dishes or cutlery. The same rule needs to be applied to your desk at work and/or at home.

- **Have mini-clutter zones:** Stock up on a few small baskets to store stray things like batteries, hair clips and other stray items that don't have a home, but may be needed again – one day!

- **Group like with like:** It's crazy to have six sets of scissors scattered throughout the house and even more crazy to own six pairs of them! You've probably bought that many because you couldn't find the other five pairs in the first place. See how being disorganised costs you money? Group things together that are for similar purposes. So put all your socks and underwear together in the same drawer. Hang all your shirts together in the cupboard. Put all your breakfast cereals together in the pantry. Group similar things together and it makes finding them a lot, lot easier.

- **Have a seasonal wardrobe:** In the first week of spring and autumn (fall), clean out your cupboards and drawers of all clothing and sports gear associated with the old season and replace with new season items. For example, in autumn pack away summer items and replace them with warm jackets, gloves etc. Store the clean, old season items in sealed boxes or a suitcase. This will mean things are always easy to find throughout the year and you're not rummaging through extra clothes looking for something to wear.

- **Set up a stationery cupboard or drawer:** If you are constantly looking for stamps, envelopes, sticky tape or pencils, then you will truly appreciate having just one cupboard or set of drawers that holds the lot. Kids can also store their craft supplies in the same place and this makes it easier to keep track of inventory and know when things need to be replaced.

- **Remove clutter storage areas:** Adding junk and clutter becomes a lot more difficult if there is nowhere to store it. Get rid of large bookcases, display cabinets, shelves and boxes as they will only attract more things to fill them up.

- **Buy multi-purpose furniture:** Use furniture that has more than one function. So, for example, buy a sofa bed so it can be used as a sofa or lounge during the day and a bed at night. Similarly, a dining room table can be also used as a desk.

- **Rent (or borrow) rarely used items:** If you are only going to use something rarely, then either borrow from friends or neighbours or rent the item. This rule applies to things like skiing and other sporting equipment, yard maintenance and other home handyman equipment.

- **Fix or throw-out broken items:** This is one of the biggest sources of clutter in most homes. Nobody wants to throw out items that look like they are easy to fix. The problem is that they are never, ever fixed and end up getting stored in cupboards or boxes in the garage. Be ruthless. If they are never going to be fixed, then they have to either be recycled or thrown out.

- **Unsubscribe from junk mail:** This applies to both physical snail mail and the ubiquitous junk emails. Every time you handle junk mail or even view junk email, you are wasting time that could be put to more productive use. Get your name off email lists by unsubscribing or marking the message as spam so it automatically gets deleted or sent to a different folder. To avoid getting your email address known by too many marketing companies, be careful about handing it out unless absolutely necessary.

Remember to keep things in perspective. There are literally thousands of articles on decluttering. It's all too easy to spend too much time reading these articles and never actually get around to doing anything. As everyone is an individual and has different circumstances, it's a far better idea to just keep things simple and experiment to find out what works best for you.

4.4 Become Super Organised

Having a tidy house where everything is easy to find is great, but why stop there when your organisation skills can soar to even greater heights!

- **Get a diary**: Buy an A4 size diary that has a page for each day and ideally is ring bound so you can tear off pages as they are used. Enter in all your appointments, reminders and birthdays.

- **Create a to-do list**: Using MS-Excel or a handy notepad, record all your tasks and reminders etc. Print the list at the beginning of each month and store it in your diary.

- **Put the weekly schedule on the fridge:** Everyone's life is ultimately focussed around the refrigerator, so they will easily get a reminder every time they open the fridge door.

- **Set up a library book box**: To avoid paying late or lost library book fines, set up a central location to store *all* books that have been read and are ready to be returned to the library.

- **Create an address book:** One of the best methods is to use a MS-Excel workbook with different worksheets for each category. For example, have one worksheet with details of essential services such as plumbers, electricians, accountant, hair-dresser etc. Then another worksheet to list contact details for friends and family etc.

- **Everything has a place**: If you are sick to death of trying to find car keys or your purse every time you go out, then set a rule that you always put essential items in exactly the same place when you come home.

- **Longer term storage**: If you absolutely can't bear to part with something, then instead of cluttering your bedroom cupboards, store the item in a separate area such as in your garage. At the end of each year, review these rarely used items and follow the de-cluttering plan rules again.

- **Handle paper once:** When bills come into the house, arrange to pay them online immediately. Scan the bill, pay the bill, record the amount in your budget spread sheet and then shred the bill. Simple. Job done! Make sure you have set up the scanner and shredder next to your computer so the job is fast, simple and efficient.

- **Reduce commitments:** If you have children, you'll quickly realise how commitments stack up. Suddenly you're on the P&C Committee and selling charity chocolates, raffle tickets and all manner of things. Combine that with driving to scouts, ballet, swimming and judo lessons and you already have a very busy life indeed. But as most people are also working full-time, this crazy schedule can become a recipe for a nervous breakdown. Prune your list of commitments, take lots of short breaks and de-schedule Sunday so it is a day of complete rest.

- **Saturday morning clean:** Start the day by doing the weekly food shopping. Head home and unpack the goods then change into your cleaning clothes and tidy up the entire house. While you are cleaning, have the washing machine working its magic. Assign each child the task of cleaning out their own rooms with the threat that you'll suck up anything left on the floor with the vacuum cleaner. Be prepared to follow through with the threat. It only takes one Barbie doll shoe to be sucked into oblivion and the offending child will never, ever reoffend!

- **Colour-code the kids:** If you have more than one child, give them a colour code. For example, give a boy the colour blue and a girl the colour pink. This will result in less fighting over lunch boxes, water bottles, toothbrushes, towels etc. Unfortunately, it doesn't solve all sibling rivalry fights, but it does take the edge off the main ones.

- **Keep an inventory list:** Not only will this be useful for insurance purposes, but it will help you focus on just how much stuff you have accumulated over the years. Keep records of how much each item cost, where it was bought and any relevant warranty periods. Take digital photos and store them with the inventory list on a memory stick and store this either at work or with another family member.

- **Create a household notebook:** Nobody does this better than www.organizedhome.com with great templates and clear instructions on how to create one.

- **Have a backup plan:** Always have alternative options available for as many disaster-prone areas of your life as possible. For example, always have spare clothes, bottled water, food, umbrellas, toilet paper, spare parking coins, first aid kit, hats, blankets, towels, socks and a small sealable plastic container stored in the back of your car. Train your children to think in a similar manner.

Golden Tip: If you plan to move house, seriously consider the benefits of downsizing and living closer to work or your children's school. The less storage you have, the less clutter you will accumulate. Use any house move as a golden opportunity to do a major decluttering of your possessions. As most removal companies charge by the box, the less stuff you have, the more money you save not just in the move, but also for your annual contents insurance policy!

4.5 Cleaning Schedule

To stay on top of the household tasks, you need to set up a regular cleaning schedule.

4.5.1 Daily Tasks

- Empty rubbish bins
- Wash dishes
- Wipe down kitchen benches
- Clean stove
- Sweep floors
- Clean bathroom
- Make beds
- Tidy living areas

4.5.2 Weekly Tasks

- Dust lights, fixtures, shelves etc.
- Scrub and disinfect toilet
- Clean and remove scum and mould from shower, bath and bathroom vanity.
- Vacuum and sweep/mop floors
- Wash, dry and iron clothes
- Spot clean walls and light switches

4.5.3 Monthly Tasks

- Wash and vacuum car
- Mow lawn, weed garden
- Remove cobwebs
- Sweep garage
- Declutter house
- Change linen and air bedding
- Clean kitchen drawers

4.5.4 Seasonal Tasks

- Change linen and air bedding
- Clean out fridge and freezer
- Heavy duty oven clean
- Check smoke detectors
- Clean windows
- Move furniture to avoid marks or fading

4.5.5 Annual Tasks

- Steam clean carpets and rugs
- Paint internal / external
- Clean out pantry
- Car servicing
- Wash curtains and blinds
- Clean gutters

5. CUTTING COSTS

"Beware of little expenses; a small leak will sink a great ship." *B. Franklin.*

5.1 Introduction

When you are going through tough times, it is essential to save money wherever possible. Sometimes, the savings come from places where you won't even notice any change in your lifestyle. Other times, it's going to take a period of adjustment as new habits are formed. The biggest budget expense for most families is for accommodation, food, transport and utility bills. Focusing on these key areas will typically result in the biggest savings.

Read through the tips and hints in the following sections and decide which ones you can implement immediately. Others tips will obviously take longer or require further research before they can be used to help reduce your expenses. Just don't give up immediately on ideas that may seem too hard. Often, with a little tweaking or discussion with family and friends, an idea that seemed impossible can become reality.

In many instances, it won't be until you get that first utility bill that you can see the fruit of your labours. Once you can physically see the bill it's much easier to understand how simple cost cutting actions really pay off! In many cases, it not only has benefits for your wallet but also for the environment. Being 'green' can be a win-win situation.

Another idea is to set yourself a challenge where you are not allowed to buy anything new (other than food and cosmetics) for an entire month. If you are up for an even greater challenge, then try doing it for one year. Aside from the green benefits to our planet, your home will also have a lot less clutter that ultimately ends up in land-fill.

5.2 Accommodation

Housing costs are typically the biggest expense most people face in their budget. Whether you are renting a property or paying off a mortgage, it is one of the biggest opportunities to turn a budget deficit into a healthy surplus. Follow these tips to cut costs:

5.2.1 Property Owner

- **Buy time:** Ask your bank for a mortgage holiday or interest only repayment schedule for whatever period you need (and can negotiate with them). This buys time to come up with a solution to your financial problems. However, be careful that this situation doesn't become ongoing and you add 10 years to your mortgage!

- **Refinance the mortgage:** Things change very quickly in the world of finance. If your mortgage interest rate is no longer competitive, then you need to shop around to find a better deal. Remember to always try and negotiate with your existing lender first as there may be financial penalties for breaking your current mortgage contract.

- **Consider selling:** If you have a mortgage over your property and the monthly repayments are more than you can afford and the situation is unlikely to improve, consider selling the property before the bank does it for you. It is always better to take action before the bank commences a mortgagee sale where you are almost guaranteed to get a lower price.

- **Rent the house:** If selling is not an option due to a depressed housing market or other valid reasons, consider renting out the property. This could be done through a property manager or directly by finding tenants yourself. If you find tenants yourself, be warned that the job is not as easy as it looks and there are all sorts of legal hurdles to jump through that you may not have realised. The rental income will hopefully make a large dent in the mortgage repayments. You can then seek out much cheaper alternative accommodation options for yourself.

- **Rent the garage:** You could rent the garage as a storage unit or it could be rented out as a car park if you live in an area where people need to park for work. Even renting out your driveway could bring in some much-needed extra cash. Check the tax and insurance situation with your accountant to make sure you meet all government rules and regulations.

- **Block split:** If you have a house on a large block of land, check with your local council to determine whether it is possible to subdivide the land. Initially this will cost you money to prepare all the required documentation, but if all goes to plan you can end up with a very nice nest egg.

- **Take in boarders**: Spare rooms should never be left empty. Instead, advertise to rent the room to a student or anyone else looking for cheaper accommodation. The extra income can be used to reduce your mortgage. Make sure to check any taxation implications before heading down this path.

- **Build a granny flat:** Again, this is something to check with the council, but there are some companies that can build a small home in your backyard that can be rented out for extra income.

5.2.2 Renting

- **Negotiate the rent**: If there is an oversupply of rental properties, leading to falling rents, makes sure you contact your landlord and negotiate for a reduction in rent. Most landlords are fully aware of market conditions and if supply is increasing while demand is falling, they will be *very* willing to keep an existing tenant – even if it means a reduction in rent!

- **Sign up in winter**: Try and ensure that you either sign a lease in winter or have it expire in winter. The reason is that less people are looking for rental properties in the colder months so there is a higher chance the rent will be reduced.

- **Work for reduced rent:** Often rental properties have maintenance tasks that could easily be performed by the tenant such as: cleaning gutters, mowing lawns or raking leaves etc. So, with a bit of negotiation a reduction in rent could be arranged in return for this work.

- **Move to a cheaper rental property:** When money is tight, sometimes you need to move to a house in a cheaper suburb or with fewer bedrooms. Enlist family and friends to help you move all your belongings in order to save on removal costs. Note that it is almost always cheaper to rent in outer suburbs and smaller towns. However, if your commuting time and transport costs increase dramatically, you need to work out the maths on whether it is actually worth it.

- **Share with more people:** Open your mind to the possibility of sharing a rental property with other family members or friends. Another option could be to rent a larger house with another family. Don't just rule out options immediately thinking, 'That would never work!' Sometimes, it could work out with a bit of flexibility and forward planning. In fact, it could work out very favourably for both parties as you could share childcare or transport arrangements – thereby only needing one car!

5.2.3 Other

- **Move in with family or friends:** Although this is undoubtedly a last option for many people, it's also a good option as family members are likely to give you more time to find your feet and come up with an alternative plan. Just don't abuse their generosity. If you are guest in someone's house regardless of your relationship to the owner, make sure you pull your weight and help out with the daily chores. If you treat their home as a hotel, the eviction notice will come that much faster.

- **Homeless shelters**: Every city will have at least one shelter. It may well mean the difference between sleeping in a bed or sleeping in a park where the potential to be robbed or assaulted is very high.

- **Buy bunk beds:** Quite simply, young children do not need to have a room of their own. Even older siblings of the same sex can easily share a room regardless of their age. Having a separate room for each child is a luxury and not a necessity. Remember that in many countries, the entire family sleeps in the same room.

- **Take on a caretaker role**: Find a job that includes accommodation as part of the benefit package. This could mean teaching in a remote location or supervising students in a boarding school. It could also be working as a caretaker for a resort or hotel.

- **Contact government services:** Get your name down for government housing benefits as quickly as possible. The waiting lists can be horrendously long, so the sooner you are on the list, the better your chances of getting subsidised housing. Alternatively, talk to church officials as often they have accommodation options that are not advertised.

- **Live in a tent**: This should only ever be a short-term option, particularly if you have children. However, it beats sleeping in a car as long as you have an air-mattress, sleeping bag and the tent is truly water proof.

- **Sell up and buy a caravan**: If times are really tough, what better way to simplify your life than to get back to basics. Sell up your house or move out of your rental accommodation and buy a caravan. This then gives you enormous flexibility in where you live. Yes, it could mean your new life resembles a travelling circus but if that means survival then you do what you have to do.

- **Sleep in the car**: Again, this is another very, very, very short-term option (i.e. one night only) and should be strongly avoided if you have young children. Make sure you park in a safe location to avoid the risk of someone breaking in and trying to steal the car while you're sleeping. A good option is near a park or shopping centre that is well lit and has toilets.

- **House-sit**: Many people going away for extended holidays or even short holidays, don't want the additional expense of pet hotels. Plus, they are mindful of security and leaving an empty house alone. This could be a prime opportunity to live in a comfortable home for a few weeks (or even months) by house-sitting their home. In return for your house-sitting duties, the owner gives you free accommodation and utility costs. This option generally works best for singles or couples without children.

- **Relocate to a different city or country:** If there are better job opportunities in a different city, state or even country, it makes sense to examine all options that you have available. Of course, this will be complicated by school-age children and other factors, but if the economic situation for your current home town is dire - then do your research and move! Just remember that if you intend to panic and uproot to a different location, make sure you do it sooner rather than later. Stampedes have a tendency to decimate property prices and if you own a property in a dying town or city, get out early to salvage what you can from a bad situation.

Golden Tip: Never, ever get yourself in a situation where you have no other option but to sleep on a park bench. Homeless people who sleep rough are at much greater risk of being robbed, raped or physically assaulted. Make sure you always have a backup plan – just in case!

5.3 Grocery Shopping

"If you make a habit of buying things you do not need, you will soon be selling things you do." Filipino Proverb

Aside from the cost of your mortgage or rent, grocery shopping is very likely to be the biggest expense to hit your budget. Although it is going to take a lot of discipline and a big change in attitude, the reward for greater savings will be well worth it. Here are at least 30 golden rules to follow when grocery shopping.

5.3.1 Before Shopping

- **Have a budget:** Using a budget spreadsheet, get to work sorting out where your money is going and how much you typically spend on grocery shopping. Take a long hard look at the shopping receipts and ask yourself, 'How much of this stuff do I really need?' You will be surprised at how much you can cut down in your weekly spending!

- **Audit the pantry:** Before putting together a meal plan, check the pantry to ensure there are no items close to their use-by date. Make sure there are always some backup meals (in a tin) that can be used in an emergency.

- **Reorganise the fridge**: Make sure the fridge and freezer are cleaned out at least once a week. Move older products to the front so they'll be used first. Work out a plan for leftovers to either eat them for lunch the next day or get creative with meals turning them into vegetable pasta bake or home-made soup.

- **Have a meal plan:** It is amazing how magazine articles often say the first step is to 'make a shopping list'. How can you do this if you haven't made a meal plan for the week ahead? Grab a good cookbook or surf the internet to get ideas for cheap, healthy dinners. Remember you want to get as many different types of fruit and vegetables into your diet as possible. A good plan is to have the last meal of the week designed to use up the last of the vegetables. This means there are no leftovers in the fridge turning into school science experiments and you get to start off the new week with a clean fridge.

- **Make a shopping list**: If you walk into the grocery store without a shopping list, then it is almost guaranteed that you will walk out with items you never planned to buy in the first place. These stores are configured by professionals. They plan the layout of the aisles so you are in their shop for as long as possible. The longer you are in there, the more chance you will spend money. Music is then carefully selected to start lulling you into a relaxed, yet upbeat and positive mood. The happier you are feeling, the more you are likely to spend. They even plant chocolate bars right at the checkout as a final temptation. It's very clever psychology at work so you need to fight fire with fire and never put one foot into that store without being prepared and holding a rock-solid shopping list in your hand. Place the shopping list on your fridge and update it as items are used up throughout the week.

- **Eat vegetarian:** Meat is expensive, so aim to eat at least one vegetarian meal each week. When you do buy meat, aim to reduce the portion size as much as possible and heap on the vegetables and pasta or rice.

- **Shop once a week (at most)**: The goal is to ensure that you only make one trip a week to the shops and have no need to top-up during the week. You'll not only save petrol by avoiding multiple trips, you'll also avoid temptation! If it is possible, try to stretch this weekly shop to every two weeks or longer.

- **Select the smallest basket/trolley:** The less space you have to hold items, the less you will buy. The idea is that you'll think twice before loading up any more goodies if there is nowhere to store them.

- **Learn to cook:** There is no point having a meal plan if you don't know how to cook. Head to the internet and do a Google search on 'how to cook'. There are some great YouTube videos and www.learnhowtocook.com has a host of recipes. Your main goal should be to eat less processed food and at least 5 different serves of fruit and vegetables every day.

- **Grow your own vegetables:** Depending on the size of your garden or even your window sill, look at your options for what you can grow yourself. You don't need much space to grow herbs, but if you have a larger section of garden, then throw on those gloves and start planting fruit and vegetables suitable for the climate and season. Ensure you have a healthy supply of soil by starting up a compost bin as well.

- **Supply your own eggs:** If your backyard is big enough and you have permission from your local council, what better way to get fresh eggs than to have your own hens! They will happily feed on vegetable scraps from the kitchen.

- **Make your own yoghurt:** There is no need to buy an expensive yoghurt making kit, instead follow the instructions on www.makeyourownyoghurt.com. Your home-made yoghurt will not only taste a lot better than the store brand; it will also be a lot cheaper!

- **Buy powdered milk:** Always have at least one packet of powdered milk on standby in your pantry. This will hopefully encourage you not to over-buy milk which is one of the most common items to be thrown out.

- **Bank emergency supplies**: Stock up on toilet paper, batteries, cold and flu medicine, matches, candles – basically anything and everything that you might run out of at 2am in the morning. If that happens, you will be forced to use a much more expensive option such as a small corner store or petrol station.

- **Choose your grocery store carefully:** Ideally go to a shopping centre which has two competing stores close to each other. At Westfield Woden (in Canberra, Australia) life doesn't get much better with a Coles right next to a Woolworths supermarket. To top it off, there is a fruit and vegetable store right between them. In this ultra-competitive environment, make sure you have no qualms with sharing your grocery bill between all three stores.

- **Form a food co-op:** Find a group of friends or work colleagues who are willing to join together and buy in bulk. A food co-op works particularly well at markets where farmers and other traders are often more willing to lower their prices for large orders. However, don't rule out the big food retailers as sometimes, with the right negotiating skills, a deal can be done.
- **Check weekly specials:** Sign up for email notifications of weekly sales items and check your mailbox for sales catalogues.
- **Combine tasks**: Don't just head off in the car to do the grocery shopping and then come home. Combine the task with filling the car with petrol, ballet lessons, school drop offs etc. The more you can squeeze into the one trip, the more petrol you will ultimately save.
- **Consider home delivery:** Depending on the distance you have to travel, the size of your shopping trolley and the number of other things you need to do, it might make sense to pay the extra for home delivery. It will also remove the temptation of buying extra items.
- **Loyalty cards and coupons**: If it doesn't cost you anything to join, then sign up for the store loyalty card and reap as many points and benefits as you can possibly muster. If you have to pay an annual fee, then think very carefully about whether you will ever get any real benefit. For example, it's no good paying $20 for a card only to find out that you need to spend $40,000 to gain enough points to get a free flight.
- **Freeze food:** To make food last longer and avoid the dreaded wastage, freeze perishable foods until they are required. This includes items such as bread, vegetables and meat. Remember that once opened, bread keeps best if you store it in an air-tight container.
- **Get creative with left-overs**: Ideally, you should have catered correctly for each meal, but sometimes food is left over. Have a plan to either eat it the next day or morph it into a soup or macaroni bake mix. Vegetables are easy to hide in another meal or alternatively give them to the chooks (hens).

- **Understand labelling:** Food can still be eaten after the 'best before' date if it is not damaged, deteriorated or perished. 'Best before' labels are commonly found on items such as cereals, sugar, flour and canned foods. However, food must **not** be consumed if it has gone past its 'use by' date. Typical types of food that have a 'use by' date are items like milk, meat and yoghurt. It can be dangerous to eat these foods if the date has expired.

- **Read catalogues:** Gather any catalogues delivered in the mail or look online to see what weekly specials are available at your local grocery stores. Stock up for the real bargains!

5.3.2 At the Shop

- **Shop with cash:** There is nothing that will focus your spending more than walking into a grocery store with cash. That's one of the reasons retailers are so keen to get you to use a credit card. If you know you have plenty of money available, are you going to knock back an extra packet of chocolate chip cookies that is not on your shopping list? To ensure you don't run out of cash, buy a cheap calculator and keep a running tally of the bill as you fill up the trolley.

- **Carry $100 bills:** It is almost impossible to buy a $2.00 raffle ticket if you are carrying cash in $100 bills as the seller usually doesn't stock enough change. Plus, people are far less likely to want to break larger notes as it means more heavy change in their wallets.

- **Leave the kids at home**: If you are brave enough to take children into the shops, you need to either have a monumental bribe in place or accept the fact you will walk out spending far more than you ever intended. If you absolutely must take the kids, then the rule needs to be 'ONE treat only' and with a rock-solid price limit. This also teaches children about budgeting and while it might be painful the first few times, the reward of well-behaved kids and a higher bank balance is ultimately worth it.

- **Use coupons:** In the USA, grocery coupons are far more popular than Australia. However, things are catching up fast and coupons are almost a necessity when buying petrol (gasoline).

- **Never shop on an empty stomach**: Make sure your stomach is filled with a hearty breakfast or lunch, and then enter the store armed with your shopping list and cash only. If you are hungry then everything will be tempting. The same rule applies if you are very tired. Most people eat more when they are exhausted so make sure you shop after a good night's sleep.

- **Manage emotions:** Never, ever shop when you are bored, rushed, stressed or the shopping centre is very crowded as you will be far more likely to make impulsive decisions that will add to your shopping bill!

- **Talk to the manager**: At a quiet time, speak to the store manager or any other staff member who looks like they know what they are doing. Ask them what day of the week is the best for specials. Also find out when the shelves are *fully* stocked. There is nothing worse than needing to make a return trip because they don't have any bread or milk in stock.

- **Buy wholesale where possible**: It can be difficult to access wholesale prices for many grocery items; however, stores such as CostCo or Aldi do allow you to buy in bulk at heavily discounted prices. Similar savings can be had at farmers' markets or even direct from local farmers. If these options are not available, ask your local grocery store manager if they can offer a better price for a much larger order.

- **Beware brand loyalty:** Many people cost themselves a small fortune by insisting their babies always wear heavily advertised nappies. Marketing companies have been very, very clever and linked the brand with the emotional heart-strings. To be fair, that's their job to be smart. However, your job is to be smarter. The store brand nappies are every bit as effective as their more expensively wrapped cousins and a fraction of the price. Open your mind to the possibility of buying a different brand – not just for nappies.

- **Buy store brands**: When there is no significant different in quality, buy generic brand items. Often, it's made in the same factory as the expensive brand product but it doesn't come with the expensive advertising and the bright, glossy packaging. You mostly can't go wrong with items such as sugar, flour, eggs, toilet paper, over-the-counter medications, milk and cleaning products. However, be careful with dairy items such as yoghurt or ice-cream which can have a nasty chemical taste!

- **Use the deli or butcher**: Meat and other small goods can be significantly cheaper at an in-store delicatessen or the local butcher. Consider also using a meat wholesaler if you have a large freezer or friends that can split the order.

- **Buy local produce**: Where possible, always try to buy food that is grown and produced locally. This not only secures jobs for people in your community, it often reduces the cost as there is minimal transportation required.

- **Buy cheaper cuts of meat**: The Australian Heart Foundation says to avoid eating processed meats like sausages, salami and ham and to limit the consumption of liver and kidneys. They suggest eating lean meat that has been trimmed of visible fat. To cut the cost further, buy cheaper cuts such as chuck steak or mince meats and use <u>less</u> than the recommended amounts in recipes.

- **Look up and down:** Have you noticed that the really cheap brands tend to be either way at the top or bottom of the shelves? Those heavily advertised brands pay a premium to be located at eye height. They are relying on the fact that people are often too lazy to look around them and reach first for that eye-height product rather than stretch up or crouch down.

- **Avoid sales assistants:** If they try to engage you in small talk you can be sure they are starting to haul in their catch. Once they make a connection with you, it can be hard to resist the sales pressure. Learn to be polite but firm in saying, 'No thank-you. Just looking.'

- **Stick to the outer edge of the store:** Fruit, vegetables, dairy and delicatessen products are usually located against walls because of the need to refrigerate these items. Processed goods are usually located in the central aisles.

- **Buy in bulk**: It's almost always cheaper to buy the larger version of a product. However, be careful that you consume it before going past the expiry date.

- **Take free samples:** If makeup counters are offering you free samples or grocery stores are offering free food samples - take them up on the offer. At the very least, it's one less mouthful of food or makeup item you need to pay for yourself.

- **Stock up at sales**: If your favourite shampoo or tinned corn is on sale, then stock up the trolley with as many items as you can afford. Just remember to check the use-by date so they don't go off before they are consumed.

- **Read the labels**: We've all been caught before with milk or yoghurt that expires the next day. That is the penalty for not checking the product more carefully before putting it into the trolley. If it's easy to reach, then grab items from the back of the shelf as they will have the longest expiry date.

- **Buy fruit & vegetables in season**: Don't try and buy mangoes in the middle of winter unless your goal is to maximise your grocery shopping bill. It's fairly easy to see what's in season as prices will come down, but as a quick guide:

  - Spring - apricots, strawberries, carrots, spinach.
  - Summer – mangoes, peaches, plums, watermelon.
  - Autumn – apples, grapes, pears, pumpkin.
  - Winter - grapefruit, lemons, oranges, turnips.

- **Buy quality over quantity**: For things that matter to you, buy quality over quantity. For example, ice-cream is a luxury item in most people's shopping trolleys. What is the point buying a large tub of generic brand ice-cream that tastes awful when you could buy a smaller container of top-quality ice-cream and really enjoy it! Frugality is not about being a cheapskate. It's about getting the best value for money and sometimes that means paying more to get a better result.

- **Reconsider buying organic foods:** Organic food is normally more expensive and if you are on a very tight budget this needs to be a more carefully considered purchase. Do the research and you are likely to find that there are already strict rules for chemical usage on non-organic products. Either way, make sure you always wash fruit and vegetables before eating them.

- **Go to the library**: Forget buying magazines and newspapers. If you have the internet or a television, then you already have access to the news. If you really need to feel paper under your fingertips, then head off to the library where it's free!

- **Choose the right checkout**: Avoid the final temptation of chocolates and lollies by choosing the confectionary-free checkout if one is available.

- **Avoid pre-cut or sliced goods**: Items that are individually portioned need to have additional packaging that adds to their cost. Never buy individually sliced or grated cheese as it will almost always be more expensive than an ordinary block of uncut cheese. Remember to store it in a sealed container in the fridge to ensure it doesn't go hard.

- **Check your docket:** You've probably read this tip before and thought, 'No way, how could they make a mistake when all they have to do is scan a barcode?' Well, it's actually very easy! Firstly, items can be double scanned. The shop assistant is almost always rushing to scan everything as quickly as possible so often they grab multiple items and end up double scanning them in the process. Secondly, items can have the wrong price matched to the barcode in the computer or vice versa. Finally, shop assistants often don't know basic fruit and vegetable names and select the wrong code.

5.3.3 Do Not Buy Items

The following items should *never* be bought as there are much cheaper alternatives available.

Item	Alternative
Garbage bin liners	Plastic bags or plastic wrapping (from toilet rolls) do exactly the same job.
Paper towels	Use tea-towels or reusable CHUX cloths to clean benches etc.
Lunch wrappers	Re-use the free plastic bags that are used for fruit and vegetables at the grocery store.
Envelopes	Keep envelopes from mail you receive and re-use them for letters you want to send out.
Air-freshener	In the toilet cubicle, light a match and blow it out to get an instant, cheap air-freshener. For other areas of the house, hunt down the source of odours rather than mask them with expensive air-fresheners.
Bottled water	Buy a re-usable bottle and drink ordinary tap water. If it's too hard or soft then get a filter.
Coffee from a café	Buy a thermos and make your own coffee at home.
Makeup remover	Good old soap and water will do a far better job for a fraction of the price. Alternatively use baby oil (which has multiple uses) to remove makeup.

Item	Alternative
Non-reusable batteries	Even though reusable batteries are more expensive, they will last longer and ultimately end up cheaper than non-reusable ones.
Grated cheese	Buy a cheese grater and do the job yourself. It's extremely easy and quick!
Pre-prepared cake mixes	This is a great marketing trick where you are really just paying for a very expensive cardboard box. Inside is a plastic bag with mostly flour, sugar and vanilla essence.
Rubbish bags	Re-use the plastic or paper bags used for groceries.

5.3.4 Fruit & Vegetable Storage

Store at Room Temperature	Ripen at Room Temperature before Storing in the Refrigerator	Store in the Refrigerator
Bananas, Grapefruit, Dry Dates, Lemons, Limes, Mandarins, Mangoes, Oranges, Papayas, Pineapple, Pomegranates, Tomatoes	Avocados, Kiwifruit, Nectarines, Peaches, Pears, Plums	Apples, Apricots, Blackberries, Blueberries, Cherries, Figs, Grapes, Moist Dates, Raspberries, Strawberries.

Store at Room Temperature	Store in the Refrigerator
Cucumber, Eggplant, Garlic, Onions, Potatoes, Pumpkin, Squash	Artichokes, Asparagus, Beans, Broccoli, Cabbage, Carrots, Cauliflower, Celery, Leeks, Lettuce, Mushrooms, Peas, Radish, Spinach, Sprouts, Sweet corn, Turnip, Zucchini.

To ensure the longest shelf life for these foods, follow these tips:

- Always store fruit and vegetables separately.
- Unless required immediately, buy fruit that isn't fully ripe.
- Do not wash fruit or vegetables until you are ready to eat them.
- Avoid cutting or trimming fruit or vegetables as they will keep much longer. If they have been cut, then make sure they are refrigerated afterwards.
- Uncut, refrigerated items should be stored in perforated plastic bags to ensure there is adequate airflow.
- Store apples and bananas away from other fruit as they release an ethylene gas which makes other fruit and vegetables go off faster.

- Conversely, to speed up the ripening of other fruit or vegetables, place them in a brown paper bag with an apple or banana. This takes advantage of the gas they emit which triggers faster ripening.
- Always remember to immediately toss out any fruit or vegetable that has gone bad as it can easily contaminate the rest of your produce. Alternatively add these items to your compost bin or give them to your chooks (hens).
- Store delicate mushrooms in a paper bag in the fridge.
- Potatoes and onions should be protected from light and stored in a cool, dark place such as a cupboard.

5.3.5 Freezer Guidelines

- Label and date every item that goes into your freezer.
- Never re-freeze food that has been defrosted.
- Avoid raw meat coming into contact with other food items by always ensuring the meat is covered.
- To avoid food poisoning, read and follow the 'Use by' labels.
- Before freezing, put meat into a bag and flatten to remove excess air.
- Check the temperature of the freezer at regular intervals to ensure it is -18 degrees Celsius.

5.3.6 Diet Tips

It takes just four weeks to lock in a new habit. Don't ever attempt to quit too many bad habits at once as you'll end up failing miserably. Aim for one new habit a month and think of the 'Hare and the Tortoise' story from childhood where a slow and steady pace ends up winning the race.

- **Quit sugar and salt:** There is a very good reason why junk food is high in sugar and salt. It's addictive. It also increases the shelf life of products so they can sit on the shelf for years without going bad. Many people think nothing of buying a chocolate bar and a soft drink as a mid-morning snack. Do the maths and you'll soon see that your little habit is costing you a *lot* of money! It's also lining your hips with wasted calories which have very limited nutritional value.

- **Know portion sizes:** It is important to educate yourself on what is the correct portion for an adult or child's meal. Read the instructions on recipes to find out how many people are really supposed to eat the meal that is being prepared.
- **Good-bye caffeine:** There's an old saying that 'coffee is your only true friend'. However, aside from making many people angry due to lack of sleep, it also ends up making many people overweight as many coffee cups are now milkshake sized and loaded to the brim in fat, sugar and mega calories. If you must drink coffee, then make sure it is decaffeinated and black (with no sugar). Otherwise you are likely to find that 'coffee is your one true enemy!'
- **Hello water**: If it has to be sayonara to caffeine, then it's a warm Caribbean-style welcome to our good, free friend – water! Drink up! Not only will your skin glow but you'll sleep better after about a week (of hell) while you withdraw from caffeine. Unless there is some compelling health reason, ordinary tap water is far cheaper than bottled water. To ensure you are not confusing hunger and thirst, have a rule that you always drink one glass of water before eating anything.
- **Eat slowly in a quiet location:** It is very hard to listen to your stomach telling you it's reached its maximum capacity when the television is blaring in the background or people are shouting. If family meals are too fraught with tension, eat your meal privately in a quiet location with no distractions. Make sure there is always a jug of water on the table for every meal.
- **Cut down on red meat**: The price of beef is escalating to new heights almost every week and the 'steak and three vegies' meal has become a luxury item for most families. That doesn't mean you have to live on lettuce and sprouts, but you need to give some consideration to switching to cheaper cuts of meat and also cutting down consumption. Try going vegetarian at least 2 or 3 nights a week. For the other 4-5 meals, look at eating more fish or chicken. Reduce the portion sizes and double up on the vegetables!
- **Understand diet-speak:** Just because a product has the words *diet* or *light* does not mean it is good for you or even low in calories. Artificial sweeteners have some frightening medical

stories - just Google 'aspartame' and 'NutraSweet' for further information. Even if the stories are exaggerated, why take the chance? Plus, if they really did work, then why is the weight loss industry thriving. Seriously, if you are going to eat something sweet make sure it is real sugar because then you can enjoy it and be satisfied by the experience rather than left feeling cheated.

- **Frozen vegetables:** If you end up each week with rotting vegetables or fruit, either get less or consider buying frozen produce. Throwing out food is really equivalent to throwing your money down the drain.
- **Make dinner in the morning** – Nobody wants to cook dinner after a long day at work. At moments like this, the temptation to eat expensive, high calorie takeaway meals will be overwhelming. To avoid falling into the trap, prepare dinner either in the morning or the night before.
- **Freeze meals** – To ensure there is always a meal on hand, double the size of the meal you have prepared and store the remainder in the freezer to eat later on in the week. This tip can also be used with left-overs to avoid wastage.
- **Use smaller crockery** – Trick your mind into thinking you have a bigger meal by using a smaller plate or bowl.

5.3.7 Cleaning Products

Watch any amount of day-time television and you'll quickly become convinced that you need a different product for every single cleaning task. It's crazy. Get back to basics and live with the germs. Just as your grand-parents miraculously managed to survive without anti-bacterial wipes – so can you! Simple products like white vinegar, bicarbonate of soda (baking soda), lemon juice and good old-fashioned soap do just as good a job. As a quick guide follow these tips for a much cheaper (and environmentally friendly) cleaning experience for your home:

- Use vinegar as a natural fabric softener by adding ½ cup of white vinegar instead of expensive brand name fabric softeners.
- Avoid the temptation of using more powder in the washing machine than what is recommended by the manufacturer. More powder doesn't necessarily mean a better wash!
- Replace ½ the amount of laundry detergent you normally would use with baking soda.
- Buy a spray bottle and fill it with 25% white vinegar and 75% water. This can then be used to clean down surfaces such as kitchen bench tops, vanity basins, windows, shower cubicles, refrigerators etc. Remember to dry windows using paper towels not newspaper. (Vinegar should not be used on aluminium surfaces or enamelled porcelain baths. Always test vinegar on a small area to ensure it is safe to use.)
- Mix baking soda (bicarbonate soda) and lemon juice into a paste to scrub soap scum marks from the bath, shower or oven.
- Place a small container of baking soda in the fridge or anywhere you need to absorb odours.
- Mop floors with a bucket of warm water and ¼ cup of dishwashing liquid. Alternatively, use warm water and 1/2 cup of vinegar. Both methods result in clean floors!

- Smelly toilets don't need expensive fragrance blocks or sprays. Instead sprinkle baking soda into the toilet bowl and leave for 10 minutes.

- Deodorise carpet by sprinkling baking soda onto the carpet. Leave overnight and then vacuum in the morning.

- Use a drop of vegetable oil on a damp cloth to shine leather shoes.

- Add a few drops of olive and lavender oil to a spray bottle filled with water. This can then be used as a cheap but very effective furniture polish. Remember to always ensure you read the manufacturer's instructions to ensure this method is appropriate.

If you can choose the floor coverings in your home, then avoid fitted carpet where possible. Not only is it cheaper to sweep a floor than vacuuming it, but there are big benefits for pet owners and families with young children. Many carpet stains have a painful tendency to be permanent and children and/or pets are particularly infamous for causing permanent, unsightly stains in highly visible areas. Try using rugs and mats instead as they are far easier to clean or replace. Homes without carpet also have benefits for asthmatics and people with other types of respiratory disorders. Other tips include:

- Ensure dish cloths stay hygienic by wetting them and placing them in the microwave for 60 seconds.

- Always clean out the microwave oven immediately after cooking as any dirt will have been softened by the heat. To remove smelly odours, fill an uncovered microwave-safe bowl with water and lemon juice and heat for 1 minute.

- Clean your oven after it has been used to keep on top of the grime and ensure it doesn't build up to scary proportions. Sprinkle a damp cloth with baking soda while the oven is still warm (not hot) and wipe down all surfaces.

- For scary ovens that haven't been cleaned in months (or years), mix ¾ cup of baking soda, ¼ cup of water and ¼ cup of salt to form a paste. Coat the inside of the oven remembering to avoid any bare metal surfaces. Leave overnight and wipe clean the next morning.

- For a few minutes every day, air the entire house including bathrooms to replace stale air and ensure mould and bacteria do not gain the upper hand.

- If your shower cubicle or bath needs super-charged cleaning, an alternative to vinegar is to buy a spray bottle and fill it with 50% bleach and 50% water. Nothing kills mould like bleach but remember to never, ever mix any other chemicals with bleach. For example, even small amounts of bleach and ammonia mixed together release a toxic gas.

- To restore a toilet bowl to its shiny old self, poor a can of flat Coke or Pepsi into the toilet and leave unflushed overnight. Once you see the results, it's unlikely you will ever drink this stuff ever again. If it can do this to a toilet, what on earth is it doing to your digestive system?

- Don't waste money buying expensive window cleaning products when methylated spirits on a cloth does a much better job. Avoid cleaning windows during the heat of the day as it causes streaks to appear as the product dries too quickly. Instead pick a cooler time during the day such as early in the morning.

- To remove stubborn stains on white clothing, rub lemon juice into the stain and allow it to dry in direct sunlight.

- Reduce the need for a major shower clean by always using a squeegee to remove soap scum and water off the tiles and/or shower door after each shower. Wash shower curtains in hot soapy water and dry in the sun.

- Ants are repelled by chalk so draw a line at their entrance to your home and watch them all head off in the opposite direction.

Golden Tip: Always start cleaning from top to bottom. So, don't start with vacuuming, sweeping or mopping until all other cleaning has been completed. Remember to always wear gloves when dealing with any chemicals.

5.3.8 Grooming

Here is yet another example of madness in our society. Do we really need a special skin cream for eyes, hands, body, face etc.? No, we don't and neither should your cosmetics budget. Back in the old days, people used to wash their hair once a week and use soap. Guess what? Soap does just a good a job of washing your hair and body as all those fancy shampoos and body washes. As for anti-wrinkle creams and potions. Get smart. Buy a good sun block, hat and sunglasses. It will achieve what no anti-wrinkle cream can do and for a fraction of the price.

Anti-wrinkle creams are really just 'hope in a jar'. The truth is that they do **not** perform the miracles the advertising industry portrays in their heavily photo-shopped images. If they did, everyone would be walking around with youthful, flawless, age-defying skin. The reality is that after you turn 40 years old, you get the skin you deserve. If you are sensible in the sun, avoid cigarette smoke, maintain a healthy diet and exercise regularly, then your chances of looking younger are much, much higher. Just remember though, that you are up against the forces of an extremely powerful industry with a seemingly infinite advertising budget. It's going to take a lot of strength and courage to resist buying that 'hope in a jar' as you get older!

Starting from top to bottom, here are over 30 tips to reduce your grooming budget but still achieve the same results:

Hair

- Avoid large hairdressing bills by keeping your hair style as short as possible. Not only will you will save money by using less shampoo, conditioner and styling products but you will save time getting ready for work or school in the mornings. Shorter hair also means you have a greater chance of being able to do free home haircuts. An added bonus is that head lice, which are in plague proportions at some schools, are less likely to make the leap to shorter hair.

- Where possible, avoid dyeing your hair. It's just another costly maintenance exercise to keep up with the regrowth. Hair dyes also damage and dry out your hair which means buying more expensive hair care products to restore the moisture balance!

- Get your partner or a friend to cut (or trim) your hair. For men and boys, an inexpensive set of electric hair clippers will pay for itself in just one or two haircuts.

- When washing hair, feel free to buy cheap store brand shampoo or use neutral pH soap for even greater savings. However, don't skimp on the conditioner as cheaper brands just won't do the job. Use a tiny amount of conditioner as only a small amount is required.

- To use up the last drop of shampoo or conditioner, leave the bottle upside down for at least 24 hours then turn back to the right side and add a little water to the container. Shake the bottle and then you will have ensured that nothing has been wasted.

- If you have very dry hair, comb through a generous amount of baby oil through your hair and leave overnight.

- Always dry your hair naturally as it will not only save electricity but also prevent your hair being damaged by the heat from the hairdryer.

Skin

- Nothing makes you look older than tired skin. Always endeavour to get at least 8 or 9 hours' sleep every night. Children obviously need a lot longer. Avoid any form of caffeine after about midday to ensure you wake up refreshed and energised for the day ahead.

- Avoid the sun in the same way people with arachnophobia avoid spiders. Never, ever sunbathe and if you live in a high UV climate, always wear high SPF sunscreen every day. Remember to wear protective clothing including a broad-brimmed hat, sunglasses and long-sleeved shirts.

- Very dry skin that is usually found on your elbows or heels is best treated by using baby oil left on your skin overnight. Use socks to prevent your bed linen getting dirty.

- Keep your nightly skincare regime as simple as possible. All you really need is a pH neutral soap such as Dove or Neutrogena to clean your face. Then follow this up with a simple moisturiser such as Carboline cream.

- Good skin needs to be hydrated and the best way to achieve this goal is by drinking 6 – 8 glasses of water every day. Avoid salty foods and caffeine in tea or coffee as they dehydrate your body.

- For daily makeup, keep things to a minimum by using a good foundation with high SPF, rouge, lipstick and eye-liner. Anything else is unnecessary or more appropriate for a nightclub. Make sure you go makeup-free at least one day of the week to let your skin breathe. This will also allow all your makeup products to last 1/7th longer! If you have good skin, consider skipping makeup entirely but always ensure you use a high SPF sunscreen.

- Store your makeup in a sealed container in the refrigerator to ensure it lasts longer.

- Use bars of soap rather than liquid products as they will last a lot longer and are usually cheaper.

- A great exfoliator can be made by mixing baking soda, corn flour or oatmeal with a little water to make a paste. Another alternative is yoghurt and oatmeal mixed together and used as a facial scrub. Use either of these recipes once a week to gain super-soft skin with a lovely natural glow.

- Yoghurt that has gone past its use-by date makes a great face mask. Leave on your skin for 5 minutes and then wash off. Honey and egg-white face masks are another popular alternative.

- A simple application of Vaseline (white petroleum jelly) will work as a cheap lip gloss and also protect against dry, wind-burnt lips.

- When your lipstick is almost finished, use a lip brush or ear bud to scoop out the remainder.

- For an instant face lift, gently steam your face over an open bowl of boiling water for 2-3 minutes. The steam hydrates your skin and gives it a youthful boost.

- Increase your Vitamin C consumption by eating more oranges and mangoes for a radiant complexion.

- To reduce puffiness and dark circles under your eyes, place cucumber slices, ice or cool tea bags over your eyes for 10-15 minutes.

Teeth

- Your teeth can be cleaned effectively by using far less toothpaste than you are probably using now. Only a small dollop is required. Many people are using about 3-4 times more than they really need.

- Always squeeze toothpaste containers from the bottom up to the top. To get the very last toothpaste out, cut the tube in half and scoop out the remaining paste. You will be surprised at how many additional brushes you can from what might have seemed to be an empty toothpaste tube.

- Reuse old toothbrushes as cleaning implements. They are great for as children's paint brushes or for cleaning fish tanks or around vanity unit taps etc.

- To get whiter teeth and remove stains, place a small amount of baking soda on a wet toothbrush. Brush your teeth as you normally would with toothpaste and then rinse. Repeat this 2-3 times a week.

- Baking soda is also great for bad breath (halitosis). If you suffer from this then dissolve one teaspoon of it in a cup of water. For best results, rinse and gargle twice a day.

- After breakfast and dinner, brush your teeth for at least 1 minute. Either set a timer or hum a song. Remember to also use dental floss for the final brush and don't be afraid to re-brush your teeth afterwards.

- To ensure you get the best result, replace your toothbrush every season and never brush too hard as this can damage tooth enamel.

Hair Removal

- Always shower or bathe before attempting to remove hair as it makes the hair softer and reduces irritation.

- Shaving is the cheapest, fastest and simplest method of removing unwanted hair on larger areas of the body. For best results, make sure that the blade is always sharp and you use shaving cream, lotion or oil. The choice of blade is a critical decision. Cheap, disposable razors will only last a short time and often have inferior results. Buy the best quality razor you can afford and then replace the blades only when necessary. Keep the blades dry as water causes them to corrode.

- Tweezers are best used for smaller areas of the body, such as eyebrows or facial hair.

- Remove hair only *when* and *where* you really need to do it. So, for example, in winter if you are female and always wearing long pants or tights, it is perfectly acceptable to let hair grow a little longer before shaving. Similarly, for men, if you are on holidays or are temporarily unemployed, save some money by growing a beard. Just remember to tidy things up before important events like dating or job interviews!

- If you have the funds available, consider permanent hair removal. Not only will it save money in the longer term but it will also save time.

General

- Consider using a roll-on deodorant in a clear container so it's easier to see when you have finished the last drop and are not throwing out product that has at least another week or two of use.

- Ask for free samples at the cosmetics sales counter or sign up for internet promotions that offer trial sizes.

- Register at a hair dressing or beauty school to get cheaper prices. Even though students will be doing the work, they will be fully supervised by professionals.

- For each grooming product, experiment with using less than what is recommended on the packaging. Often you will find that 'less' does the job just as effectively as 'more'.

- Shop online or at discount pharmacies for even greater savings.

- Tip containers upside down to ensure that every last drop has been used.

- These are tough times - remember that you do not **need** perfume, scented talcum powder, bubble bath or nail polish.

5.3.9 Pets

Unfortunately, this is a big dilemma for many people who are struggling to make ends meet. This is a highly emotional topic as most people consider their pets to be family members. But sometimes in life you have to make tough decisions in tough times. If you absolutely have to do it, make sure your pet goes to a good home and contact the local RSPCA or animal refuge for advice. Never, *ever* abandon a pet. However, if you already have a pet and cannot bear to part with them, follow these tips to reduce the cost:

- **Use generic foods:** Your pet is never going to know the difference between generic (or store) brand food and the more expensive label brands.

- **Register your pet:** To avoid expensive fines, make sure your pet is correctly registered with the local council.

- **Buy insurance:** If your pet became seriously ill or injured then you need to decide what level of treatment you can afford. Some veterinary bills are horrendously expensive and having pet insurance can give you a lot more options.

- **Health checks:** Many pets have a regular schedule of veterinary checks and injections that are required for them to maintain good health. Skipping things like heart worm tablets for your dog could leave them open to a pretty horrific death.

- **Holiday care:** To avoid kennel or cat boarding fees, arrange for family or friends to look after your pet if you are away from home. This could also be another short-term option if you are having financial difficulties.

5.4 Utilities

If you have reached the point where you dread receiving another utility bill, now is the time to fight back and work out a plan to cut costs. Just simple changes in how you live can make a massive difference and turn what used to be a horrible shock into a pleasant surprise.

5.4.1 Cut Electricity Costs

- **Turn off the lights:** It is amazing how many people fail to turn off lights in their house when they leave a room. Some households seem to be making a valiant attempt to replicate a lighthouse. Unfortunately, these people are going to face the economic equivalent of an electric shock when they get their electricity bill. Train everyone to turn off the light when they leave a room.

- **Use candles:** If you don't have young children and your budget is really, really tight then consider using candles at least for some of the time. Note that this tip comes with a very strong warning as candles are the cause of many household fires. Please read these safety rules before lighting any matches - www.candles.org/safety_rules.html.

- **Sleep with the sun:** Change the hours you sleep to match what is happening outside. Don't sleep in during the morning when the sun is up and stay up late when the sun is down. Similarly, don't wait until it is dark before cleaning the house or getting the children to do their homework or have showers. Aim to have as many chores completed before the 'free' lights go out!

- **Turn off the mains:** Going away for a holiday? Make sure you have whittled down the food in the refrigerator to nothing so that you can turn off the electricity at the main supply while you are away. You won't add a cent to your electricity bill while you are away.

- **Shop around for better deals:** If you have the opportunity to change energy providers, then phone around to see which one offers the best deal for your household. At the very least, contact your current provider and make sure you are on the most cost-effective plan.

Country	Sample Website(s) *Remember to check the internet for even more websites*
Australia	www.myenergyoffers.com.au www.energywatch.com.au www.yourchoice.vic.gov.au www.youcompare.com.au
New Zealand	www.powerswitch.org.nz
United Kingdom	www.ukpower.co.uk www.theenergyshop.com www.uswitch.com
USA	www.saveonenergy.com www.moveutilities.com

- **Learn to read the meter:** This is the equivalent of learning to read a sales invoice. It is the numbers that the electricity company uses to work out your energy bill. Get to know this meter like your best friend and you'll gain a good understanding of what causes the numbers to go higher. It also teaches you the location of the main supply switch which is important for safety reasons.

- **Switch off appliances:** Do you leave the television, microwave, computer, washing machine and other electrical equipment on stand-by mode throughout the day? This is called 'vampire drain' and if you switch off these power sucking devices at the wall you can save approximately 10% of your annual electricity bill for the year. This works out to be around $10 per year for each appliance. To make the task easier, consider using power strips so one flick of the switch turns off three or four electrical appliances at the same time. Alternatively use a standby power controller (SPC) which automatically switches off appliances when they are not being used.

- **Ditch the clothes dryer:** If the weather is amenable, use the sun to dry your clothes for free. If not, then dry clothes indoors near a heater (that's already on). Be careful never to hang clothes over electrical appliances as this is a common cause of house fires. If you do need to use a clothes dryer, make sure you remove lint from the filter so it operates more efficiently. Clean out the lint vent regularly to improve the dryer's performance and give clothes an extra spin in the washing machine beforehand so less drying time is needed.

- **Good-bye electric hairdryer, curling wand or straightener:** Have a shower at night and your hair will dry naturally as you sleep. Find a hairstyle that doesn't need any blow-drying, curling or straightening to look good. In general, the less hair you have the better, as longer hair is higher maintenance. In general, if you embrace your natural hair type and don't try and work against it, your hair will become your crowning glory.

- **Sell off the spare fridge:** If you have a second fridge or freezer, consider selling it on EBay (or through a garage sale). Not only will you get extra cash but you'll also save electricity!

- **Look for the energy stars:** If it's time to replace electrical items, look for the most energy-efficient ones with highest number of yellow stars. Avoid buying cheap electric fan heaters as they are usually much more expensive to run than oil heaters. Front-loading washing machines and fridges with the freezer compartment at the top are also more energy efficient.

- **Buy the right size appliances:** If you have a large family and buy a small washing machine, you will ultimately need to do more loads to achieve the same result. This will end up costing <u>more</u> money.

- **Install energy saving light bulbs:** Compact fluorescents light (CFL) bulbs last up eight times longer than ordinary incandescent light bulbs and are significantly cheaper to run.

- **Use motion-sensor lighting**: Instead of having outdoor security lighting on throughout the night, install motion-sensor lighting.

- **Charge your phone or laptop at work:** If your job requires you to use a mobile phone or laptop, then it's only fair that your employer also pays for the battery to be recharged.

- **Operate your fridge efficiently:** Limit the number of times you open the door and set the temperature as follows: fridge at 4°C, freezer at -18°C. Make sure that the fridge or freezer is not placed directly next to an oven or stove as more energy will be required to keep things cool. Ensure that the fridge and freezer are around three quarters full but not overloaded.

- **Clean refrigerator coils**: The fridge is one of the most expensive electrical appliances to run, so it is important that it runs as efficiently as possible. Every couple of months, turn off the fridge and vacuum the refrigerant coils located either at the back or underneath the unit. Consult your fridge operating manual for further maintenance instructions.

- **Defrost food in the fridge:** The most hygienic and energy efficient way of defrosting food is to do so in the fridge. Not only does it help cool other items in the fridge compartment, but it saves wasting electricity by using the microwave oven. Never defrost food in warm or hot water as this allows bacteria to grow on the outer surface of the food.

- **Limit television & internet usage:** Do you really need to watch television every single night? Will your life come to a standstill if you don't check your email or Facebook account? The answer is a resounding 'No!' Life will go on and you will be grateful for the smaller numbers on your electricity bill and the extra time you have to pursue more worthwhile, income-producing activities.

- **Use human power over electrical power:** Leaves can be swept up with a broom rather than using an electric blower or vacuum. Similarly, electric can openers and knives can be replaced with manual devices.

- **Turn off the electric garage door:** Life is so convenient when you can drive home from work and press a little button and the garage door opens magically. However, this so-called convenience is a really big power drain and the exercise you get by jumping out of the car to open or close the garage door will also help you burn off calories.

- **Consider solar power:** Yes, you will need a calculator for this task but if it pays off in a reasonable amount of time (and you live in a sunny climate) it may well be worth it. A solar hot water system can save at least 50% off your hot water heating bill.

- **Install a skylight:** If you find that you constantly need to have a light turned on in the kitchen, installing a skylight or solar tube in the roof can help solve the problem.

- **Painting walls in lighter colours:** A room painted in dark colours will always seem darker regardless of the time of day. Avoid feature walls as they often are painted in darker colours.

- **Use the microwave:** It is cheaper to use the microwave or a gas grill rather than an electric oven.

- **Avoid opening the oven:** Each time the oven door is opened unnecessarily the temperature drops by up to 15 degrees Celsius which means more energy is required to recover from the drop.

- **Get on the right plan:** Most energy providers have different plans depending on your usage patterns. Make sure you are on the most efficient plan by phoning your provider and asking them how you can reduce your consumption. Some electricity plans have off-peak pricing and you can reduce your bill further by doing simple things like washing clothes outside peak times.

- **Investigate government grants:** Many government agencies have grants and rebates on offer for people that install energy efficient devices.

- **Reduce ironing time:** Try and buy clothes that don't need dry-cleaning or ironing. For clothes that do need ironing, make sure they are hung in the bathroom as the steam from a hot shower will help remove wrinkles. The less wrinkles, the less ironing that is required.

- **Iron efficiently:** After turning on the iron, items that require a hotter setting should be done first. Any clothing that requires a cooler setting should be done after the iron has been turned off. This saves wasting energy (and time) waiting for the settings to change.

- **Cook on free council barbeques:** Many local parks in Australia have free gas barbeques. These are predominantly used on weekends particularly for parties, but there is nothing to stop people using them throughout the week.

- **Prepare for electrical storms**: If there is a storm with lightning, make sure you turn off and <u>unplug</u> all electrical appliances. If you house gets struck by lightning then anything plugged in to the socket will get zapped. This can happen regardless of whether the switch is turned on or off.

5.4.2 Cut Heating Costs

"Chop your own wood and it will warm you twice." - Henry David Thoreau.

- **Dress for the cold:** If you live in a cold climate then dress for the cold. That means wearing jumpers, thermal underwear and warm pants both inside and outside. If you like to walk around the house in the middle of winter and dress like it is summer, then be prepared to fork out a fortune for the privilege.

- **Turn off the heaters:** This is not rocket science. If you are not going to be at home during the day, make sure that all the heaters and any other appliances are turned off at the wall. If you've dressed warmly and insulated your house, then heaters should only be run for very short periods while you are at home. Make sure they are adjusted to give a room temperature no greater than 20 degrees Celsius. Unless you live in Siberia, heating should also be turned off at night when you're safely tucked up in bed with plenty of blankets.

- **Heat only one room:** A house with ducted heating and cooling that cannot be zoned is a house with a BIG electricity bill. Why pay to heat or cool an entire house? It's pure insanity! Far better to turn off the central heating and warm up the family room with a single, energy-efficient oil (or gas) heater. Close off sections of the house that are not being used by shutting doors. Remember to place the heater away from the windows to ensure more heat is distributed around the room.

- **Lower the thermostat:** If you have central heating, a pleasant room temperature is around 21 degrees Celsius. However, if you dress warmly you can easily lower it a further one or two degrees to cut between 10% and 20% from your heating bill.

- **Lower the water temperature:** Turn down the thermostat to around 60 degrees Celsius. Consider switching to natural gas or solar hot water as it can pay for itself within a few years. Whatever you do, aim to ensure you are not paying to heat water so you can enjoy a piping hot shower at 2am in the morning. If you live in a very hot climate, consider turning off the hot water system completely in summer. A further benefit is that cold showers end up being quick showers - which will also save on water costs.

- **Insulate the water heater**: Surround the water heater system with additional insulation to help retain heat and improve the efficiency.

- **Drink warm beverages:** Nothing warms you up like a nice hot cup of chocolate, tea, coffee or home-made soup. Make sure you don't overfill the kettle by only heating the water you require.

- **Cook up a feast:** Gather everyone into the kitchen and give them hot beverages while the oven is heating up the room cooking dinner (or lunch).

- **Exercise:** A good brisk walk or run around the block will not only burn up a few hundred calories, it will also improve your blood circulation and warm you up. If it is too cold to go outside, then compromise by doing 50 star jumps in the lounge room. Just make sure to check with your doctor before undertaking any vigorous exercise as a heart attack is not part of the plan for 'warming up'.

- **Warm up your bed:** It might seem ludicrous to suggest the obvious, but load up your bed with layers of blankets and doonas. Before you go to bed, place a hot water bottle under the covers and you'll be toasty warm. Don't even think about using an electric blanket!

- **Block draughts:** Use door snakes (or rolled up towels) to block draughts and hang thick curtains with a pelmet overhead to block cold air coming in through glass. If you get condensation on your windows it's because the glass is not providing an effective seal against the outside elements. If replacement isn't an option, consider using bubble wrap as a shield against the cold. Find further information by going to YouTube to see videos demonstrating how to do it.

- **Insulate your home:** This may not be possible if you are renting or if money is really tight, but it's worth doing the maths to see what the savings could be in the longer term. This might include options such as installing aluminium roller shutters (also known as honeycomb blinds) on windows that don't face the street. Alternatively, replace window panes with double glazing or consider the cheaper alternative of secondary glazing (fitting a membrane to the window) instead. A home that is properly insulated can save up to 20% on heating and cooling costs.

- **Let there be light:** And there was – well, once plants were pruned that were blocking light entering the windows. In cold weather, open the curtains during the day to let the heat from the sun into the house. At night, close all the curtains to trap as much heat inside as possible.

- **Make use of mirrors:** A cleverly positioned mirror can reflect light making the darkest room seem instantly lighter.

- **Position furniture correctly:** This may seem obvious, but don't place furniture against windows so that it blocks light coming into the room. If you are buying new furniture, opt for lighter coloured furniture, particularly if the room it will be placed is mostly in shade during the day.

- **Grow deciduous shrubs and trees:** In summer, the thick foliage from deciduous trees and shrubs will block the sun's heat. In winter, as the leaves have died off, the sun can shine through to heat up the house.

- **Turn off gas pilot light:** In summer when gas heaters are never used, make sure you turn off the pilot light.

- **Close your fireplace:** Remember to close the furnace door when not in use to stop cold air entering the house.

Golden Tip: Spend as much time as possible at a friend's house or go to the library where heating (and cooling) is free. The *less* you are actually in your home, the *less* money you'll spend on heating and cooling.

5.4.3 Cut Cooling Costs

- **Shut out the light:** If it's going to be a hot day, then prepare early and close all curtains and blinds to prevent heat entering the house.

- **Consider tinted windows:** Again, this is another tip that will require a calculator, but if you live in a warm to hot climate, it may pay to get windows tinted to reflect the glare and heat of the sun.

- **Use fans in place of air conditioning:** Electric fans will cool a person not a room. So, make sure you are actually in the room with the fans going and don't leave them on thinking they will cool the room on their own. Fans use 1/10th of the power of air-conditioning. On a hot day choose wisely.

- **Clean air-conditioning units**: The air filters of air-conditioning units need to be cleaned on a monthly basis. This is because the more dust they harbor, the less efficiently they work. Make sure outside units are clear of any obstructions that may prevent them working properly. Also set the fans to high speed to ensure the unit is operating at its highest efficiency. Make sure the air conditioning unit is placed on the shadiest side of the house.

- **Limit heat-generating appliances:** If cooking up a storm heats up your kitchen, it makes sense to avoid doing this during the hottest part of the day!

- **Turn up the air-conditioning unit**: Raising the temperature by one degree Celsius will reduce the electricity consumed by 10%. Set the thermostat to 24 degrees Celsius to ensure the air-conditioning doesn't come on unless absolutely necessary.

- **Drink cold drinks:** This is a no-brainer. If you sip iced-water or tea then you'll start to feel cooler. Make sure that if you are not at home that you carry your own water bottle to avoid buying expensive, environmentally friendless bottles of water.

- **Dress for the heat:** Common sense tells you that the less you wear inside, the cooler you will become. In the comfort of your own home, there are no rules that say you can't get about in your underwear!

- **Take a cold shower:** Nothing will lower your temperature faster than a cold shower on a scorching hot day. Better yet, get ice cubes in a towel and wrap them around your head.

5.4.4 Cut Water Bills

- **Wash with a full load:** Set the washing machine to cold water and load up to the top level. Always avoid washing just one or two items. It's a major waste of water and electricity. Remember to turn off the power at the switch and make sure you also turn off the taps! This is because the hose connecting water to the machine can burst causing thousands of dollars in water damage. Ensure that you use the shortest possible cycle option on your washing machine. There is nothing to be gained by over-washing your clothes.

- **Wash only dirty clothes:** Some people want pristine perfection in their clothes every day and that's fine if you are going to wear those clothes to work. However, if you're just going to wear clothes around the house you really don't need to be so perfect. Besides, clothes like jeans tend to look better when they are a little dirty. Just don't tip the balance by falling into 'scruffy' and remember - it's a fine line!

- **Avoid cigarette smoke**: If you intend going out after work, re-think the clothes that you wear if you intend going into an environment where people are smoking. Your clothes will absorb the odour and it will be very hard to remove it without washing or dry-cleaning the garments.

- **Buy a water-efficient washing machine:** Look for the energy star rating sticker on a front-loading machine and aim for the highest number of stars.

- **Install water saving devices:** A water-saving shower head costs around $35.00 (in Australia) and will end up paying for itself in no time. If you have a larger budget, consider installing a rainwater tank.

- **Shower at work:** If your workplace provides a shower for employees, then you are insane not to use it. Not only is it free water but it reduces your water heating costs as well. An even better plan is to exercise in the morning before going to work and then have your daily shower afterwards when you get to work.

- **Skip a shower/bath:** If you know you won't be going out anywhere on the weekend, skip the Friday night shower and instead give yourself a hospital-style sponge bath.

- **Cut your hair:** The longer your hair, the longer it takes to wash and the more water you use in the shower. You also need more shampoo, conditioner and styling products. Learn to cut your own hair or get family members to do it for you.

- **Share the shower:** At least once a week (if not more), share the shower or bath. If you have young children (under 5 years old) then they should be sharing the bath or at least re-using the water, all the time. Showers use only a third of the water and power needed for a bath. Remember to keep a window slightly open during the shower to avoid moisture forming. This is particularly important in winter as dry air is easier to heat.

- **Wash underwear in the shower**: Use underwear to block the drain and create a mini-bath in the shower. As you wash your hair and body, use the soap suds to clean your underwear at the same time. Hang items up in the shower to dry. This tip saves on water costs and extends the life of delicate clothing.

- **Shower and clean at the same time:** While you are waiting the recommended 1-2 minutes for conditioner to stay on your hair, use that time to quickly clean down the shower cubicle. A quick clean each week and your shower will always be mould and grime free.

- **Buy an egg timer:** Strip off, tip up the egg timer and jump into the shower. Make sure you have everything you need such as soap and shampoo as you only have 4 minutes to get clean and not a second longer! Challenge yourself to do it in 3 minutes for even greater cost savings.

- **Re-use bath water**: Don't let this precious, expensive water go to waste. Instead use it to hand wash delicate clothes such as underwear or woollen jumpers. Afterwards, place a bucket beside the bath and scoop water out to flush the toilet throughout the day.

- **Sit in the bath while it fills**: If the bath water is running while a person is sitting in the bath, their body will displace the water and less water will be used to fill the bath. Never, ever run a bath when there is nobody sitting in it and only fill it up to ¼ the height of the bath.

- **Check all plugs for leaks**: A leaky plug is a silent water snatcher. Check for leaks by leaving the plug in the hole for 10 minutes after being used. If the water level has reduced, the plug is leaking.

- **Use the pool:** If your children have swimming lessons or you are going there to cool off and/or exercise, try and get an afternoon session. Afterwards make sure the kids (and yourself) take a shower, as it will cut about $1/10^{th}$ of your water bill each week plus save on water heating costs.

- **Shower before bed:** Change your schedule so that you shower at night instead of in the morning. This will mean your bed linen should remain fresh and clean for a lot longer. It will only need to be washed on a monthly basis rather than every week!

- **Catch wastewater:** If your hot water takes ages to come through in the shower, then catch the wastewater in a bucket and use it on the garden or to flush the toilet.

- **Reduce toilet flushing:** There's an old saying, 'If it's yellow, let it mellow. If it's brown, flush it down.' Quite simply, it is not necessary to constantly flush the toilet at home especially if it is being used frequently.

- **Wash dishes by hand**: Fill up the sink with hot water and washing up liquid. Soak the dishes so they mostly wash themselves and then place them in the dish rack to air-dry. Dishwashers should only be used if you have a full load and no time to hand wash. Ensure that you use the economy cycle and turn off the dry cycle to save even more energy.

- **Fix leaking taps:** Either get a plumber in or learn to do it yourself because leaking taps use up far more water than you can ever imagine. Instructions on how to do it can be found at www.howtoaustralia.com.au/indoor/a_guide_to_fixing_a_leaking_tap.

- **Brush teeth with the taps off**: There is no reason whatsoever to run the taps while you brush your teeth. It is literally washing money down the drain. If you are waiting for the water to heat up (so you can wash your face), catch the water in a cup so you can use it to rinse your mouth after brushing your teeth.

- **Rinse razors in the sink:** Again, when shaving facial hair, it is important not to rinse the razor in running water. Instead, fill up the sink with a small amount of warm water and use this to clean off the blades.

- **Re-use towels:** Remember that you live in a home not a hotel. Assign everyone in the family their own towel and make sure it's hung up to dry after each use. Unless exceptionally dirty, they should only need washing once a week.

- **Smart kettle usage:** Only fill the kettle with as much water as you need. Limit the number of hot drinks you have in hot weather as they will do nothing to keep you cool.

- **Install a water tank**: If it is possible to fit a rainwater tank to your home, it may well work out to be a very cost-effective measure.

Check government regulations to see if you are entitled to a rebate.

- **Avoid using garbage disposal units**: If you have one installed, there is no reason to use it as food should not be washed down a sink. Instead it should be placed in a compost bin, fed to the chooks or placed in the rubbish bin for domestic waste.

- **Train your kids:** It is a very simple lesson to teach children that taps always need to be fully turned off after use. Always explain to them the reasons for any rule you set as it helps them understand <u>why</u> you are doing it.

- **Drain the swimming pool**: Many councils charge additional water fees for properties that have a pool. Aside from the extra waters cost there are also maintenance and safety issues that need to be constantly addressed. In tough times, a swimming pool is a luxury that simply cannot be justified. However, filling in the pool is a very expensive exercise. One of the best options is to drain the pool and install a deck over it. This means that when you come to eventually sell the property, it can be sold with (or without) the benefit of an in-ground pool. The empty space underneath the deck can also be used for storage.

- **Check for hidden leaks**: Check the water meter at the beginning and end of a two-hour period when no water is being used by the household. If there is any change in the reading, then there is a leak.

- **Smart car washing**: Always use a sponge and bucket to wash down your car as a hose typically uses 4 to 5 times more water. To avoid run off <u>and</u> water the grass, ensure your car is washed on the lawn and ideally in the shade to avoid streaks on the paint as the car dries. Note that it is important to use garden friendly cleaning products so you don't kill off the lawn.

- **Clever gardening:** Add mulch to your garden to help the soil retain moisture and lessen the amount of watering that is required. Grow plants that are native varieties as they will best match the climate and thrive with less effort. If you have a large garden, then consider installing a drip irrigation system. Never, ever water plants in the heat of the day as you can kill them and water will be wasted by evaporation. Instead water plants in the early morning or late evenings.

To encourage plants to grow deeper roots and hence need less frequent watering, water the garden for longer periods but less often. A good rule of thumb is to put an empty can of tuna on the grass and when it's full of water then you have completed your 'deep watering' of the garden.

- **Consider water recycling systems**: Contact your plumber for advice on installing a grey water reuse system in your home. Waste water from the bathroom and laundry can be reused on the garden. Care must be taken though with the cleaning products used in these areas.

- **Sweep the driveway**: In the olden days, many people used to clean their driveways with a hose wasting an enormous amount of water. To avoid a massive stress-induced headache when you receive your water bill, make sure you use a broom to sweep leaves and dirt from your driveway.

- **Collect rainwater**: Even if you do not have a rainwater tank, you can collect rainwater in buckets and other containers as it flows out the down spout. Later on, this water can be used on the garden or to flush the toilet.

- **Re-use cups**: Assign everyone a cup for the day and get them to re-use it for drinking water, tea or other beverages. This means that your sink will not be filled with a multitude of cups that all need to be washed.

Golden Tip: One of the best websites for information on saving water is www.savingwater.com.au. Aside from hundreds of water saving tips, it also has a range of helpful videos explaining how to perform basic water saving tasks. Online tutorials show viewers how to replace a showerhead and tap washer along with how to check for leaks and install a water flow controller.

5.5 Transport

Most people that have never tracked their spending are going to be in for an almighty shock once they realise how much money they are spending on transport. It is likely to be a significant and unexpected hit to their budget plans.

5.5.1 Smarter Travelling

- **Perform an audit:** Sit down and work out all the trips your household makes throughout the week. Often you will find that many things can be combined in the one trip. So, for example, if you are taking your children to swimming lessons it could be a great opportunity to do the weekly food shopping at the same time. It's called 'killing two birds with the one stone' and if you are serious about slashing your budget, you need to start thinking of different and cheaper transport options that could work for your family.

- **Move house:** After your transport audit, it may be apparent that you are living in the wrong house. If it's possible to rent or buy a house closer to your children's school (or your work place) and the cost of doing so is less than what you are paying now, then moving house is a no-brainer.

- **Use public transport:** If the service is safe, reliable and located close to your destination, then consider using public transport as it is almost always going to be cheaper than buying a car. Take this exercise one step further and buy cheaper season or monthly tickets (where they are available).

- **Ride the school bus:** If it works out cheaper, then put your kids onto the local school bus. Not only does this increase their independence, it will also increase your bank balance and save you time.

- **Apply for concession cards:** Many bus and rail companies offer concession cards for a variety of situations including people who are unemployed.

- **Travel off-peak:** Look out for discounted public transport tickets when you travel outside peak hours. If possible, arrange to work at a different time to capture these savings.

- **Find your feet:** Nothing moves the pounds (or kilograms) faster than walking. What better way to make it part of your daily routine than to have it as your source of transport? There are just so many health benefits from walking that it's truly surprising that government health departments haven't started a campaign to get more people walking to work. Remember to always get a medical check done by your doctor prior to commencing any new exercise regime.

- **Buy a bicycle:** Many large cities have installed an extensive network of bike paths. If you are physically able to pedal a bike to and from work, then buy yourself a bike (and helmet) and get pedalling. The other alternative is to buy a motorised bicycle and then a whole new world opens up as longer commuting distances will then be possible.

- **Consider a motor bike:** In Asia, most people with motorised vehicles get around quite happily on a motor bike or scooter. If the roads you are travelling are not high-speed highways and you are mainly limited to low speed, quiet streets, then a motor bike will be a lot cheaper to run than a car.

- **Carpool:** Put a sign up on your office noticeboard or ask friends and family if anyone wants to share their car (and running costs) for the daily trip to and from work.

- **Cut activities:** If you or your children are doing multiple extra-curricular activities, work out which ones are the most transport-efficient for your household and consider dropping those that are not truly needed.

- **Run only ONE car:** Many people think that families need two (or more cars) in order for them to go about their daily tasks. If you are running more than one car per household, then you are simply not trying hard enough to cut your expenses. Do the maths on the running costs i.e. insurance, maintenance, petrol, loan repayments, license costs and capital loss on the purchase price of the vehicle. Then compare these costs with using a taxi or bus. You should find selling the second car a very easy decision.

As an example, in Canberra, Australia it currently costs $2.65 for a pre-paid MyWay ticket to travel during peak hours. (This excludes the 5% discount by paying via BPay or direct debit.) To make calculations easier, let's just say it's roughly $5.00 a day to catch the bus to and from work.

Contrast this figure with the cost of driving to work where parking is around $10.00 a day. Average petrol costs are around $8.00 a day when travelling from a middle ring suburb. Car registration and insurance are estimated at around $4.00 per day. Car maintenance is estimated at around $1,000 per year for things like servicing, new tyres etc. which equates to around $2.70 per day. This all comes to an approximate (and conservative) estimate of $25.00 a day compared to the $5.00 a day bus fare. Oh, and that's not even taking into account any car repayments or depreciation of the 'asset'. Quite simply, it would be cheaper to use public transport during the working week and hire a car every second weekend. So, ask yourself again, "Do we really **need** a second car for our household?"

- **Shop around for rental cars:** Use the internet to hunt down the best deals and don't be afraid to ask for a free upgrade or discount for repeat business. Remember to carefully check the rental car insurance contract as your credit card may already cover the insurance.

5.5.2 Cut Car Running Costs

- **Buy a second-hand vehicle:** Never, ever buy a new car unless of course you are rolling in so much cash that it doesn't matter. Instead, buy a good second-hand vehicle which is at least 2 years old with low mileage, high fuel efficiency and ideally still within the manufacturer's warranty period. If you do buy a new car, the moment you drive it out of the car sales yard, it drops immediately in value. Why pay for nothing just to get that new car smell of fresh plastic and paint? If you have young children, a new car means nothing to them. Within the blink of an eye, your brand-new car will be christened with baby vomit, spilt milk or something sticky that you never expected. Stains and scratches will show up regularly and you'll realise very quickly that the new car smell wasn't really worth it.

- **Beware brand snobbery:** Remember that your car is needed to get you safely from point A to point B. It should not be used as a fashion statement or to maintain a social status which is beyond your bank balance. It's a well-known fact that many billionaires drive understated, late-model cars that they have owned for many years. In tough times, you don't want to be a target for thieves by parking an expensive car outside your home.

- **Remove heavy items:** Every 25 kilograms of additional weight increases the amount of fuel used by around 1%. This includes roof racks which create an air drag for the car.

- **Buy a smaller car:** It is common sense to realise that a bigger car costs more to run than a smaller car. Always check the cost of maintenance, licensing, insurance and fuel consumption before buying a car. Plus ensure it has received a full vehicle inspection by a qualified, independent mechanic. If you do end up getting a new car, buy it at the end of the year as dealers try to offload vehicles before they become "last year's model".

- **Rotate car tyres regularly:** At least every four months, move your car tyres into a different position. They will last longer if you rotate them regularly.

- **Find a good mechanic:** Use word of mouth to find a good mechanic that can service and repair your car without ripping you off. Regularly servicing your car will ensure that small problems do not become big problems.

- **Conduct proper maintenance:** Follow the owner's manual to ensure your vehicle is operating in the most efficient manner possible. Check your tyre pressure levels every month to ensure they are fully inflated as underinflated tyres add rolling resistance. To gain an accurate reading, make sure you measure the pressure when the tyres are cold. Also, make sure that your tyres are aligned properly and air filters are cleaned regularly.

- **Learn basic skills:** Ensure you are able to change the car oil or replace a flat tyre. This will save the cost of someone else doing it for you.

- **Avoid rapid stopping & starting:** Driving too close to car in front is a recipe for a rear-end accident. Sadly, too many drivers learn this basic lesson the hard way and pay dearly for the consequences. The faster you accelerate from a stop position, the more fuel that is consumed. A good rule of thumb is to always drive as if you are heading to a dentist appointment.

- **Use gears correctly**: For manual transmission cars, change up to a higher gear as soon as possible. For automatic cars, ease back slightly on the accelerator once you have reached your desired speed.

- **Drive at a slower speed**: There are substantial savings in petrol if you drive at a slower speed and use cruise control. This applies particularly on longer trips where a 5 mph (8 km/hr) reduction in speed can reduce fuel consumption by 7%. However, don't use cruise control in mountainous areas as it will be less efficient.

- **Time the lights:** To avoid unnecessary stopping and starting, get to know the cycle of traffic lights on your regular commute in order to have a more fuel-efficient journey to work.

- **Limit the use of heating or cooling:** Running the air-conditioning or heating is not free, so limit the use just as you would in your home. If you are travelling at speeds less than 60 km/hr, open a window to cool down. For higher speeds, use the air-conditioning but make sure all the windows are closed.

- **Stay at home day:** Have one day a week, usually Sunday where you stay at home and don't spend any money travelling anywhere. This is the day where you actively plan to spend nothing and minimise your utility costs as well.

- **Cruise down hills:** Be aware of your surroundings and take your foot off the accelerator as much as possible when you are going down hills. Maintain momentum by timing the lights so you avoid the need to come to a complete stop. However, don't use 'angel gear' (neutral) when going down hills as it is very dangerous.

- **Do not idle unnecessarily:** If traffic is going nowhere in a hurry, then consider shutting down the engine if you will be stopped for one minute or longer.

- **Follow the rules:** Speeding and parking tickets can put a serious, unexpected dent in your budget. Far worse is driving under the influence of alcohol or drugs as this can result in prison sentences. It's always better to follow the road rules, drive to weather conditions and keep out of trouble!

- **Shop around for car insurance:** Never, ever automatically renew an insurance policy without making at least three phone calls to alternative insurance companies. Afterwards go back to your current insurance company and ask for a discount to match your best quote.

- **Use coupons when available:** Always keep a stash of petrol coupons in your car glove box to ensure that you get the cheapest deal on offer when you buy fuel for your car.

- **Monitor the petrol price:** Keep track of daily petrol prices for at least a month to determine if there is a pattern to petrol prices in your area. Remember that driving for 10 minutes to save $2.00

in petrol is false economy as you will have spent more in petrol usage than the savings to be gained. Have a chat to the petrol station assistant and ask them which days of the week the petrol price is usually the cheapest.

- **Escape peak hour:** The more stop-start driving that you do, the higher your fuel bill. If possible, schedule your trip for outside the peak hours of 8.00am - 9.00am and 4.00pm-6.00pm.

- **Fill up efficiently**: Each time you fill up the car on petrol (gasoline), make sure you completely fill the tank. This lowers the risk of needing to keep driving to the petrol station multiple times throughout the week. It also prevents you running out of petrol in an unsafe area. Alternatively, if your normal route involves passing a petrol station on a regular basis then only fill up when the price dips throughout the week, but never go below ¼ full.

  Always fill up the tank early in the morning when the temperature is still cool. As the temperature rises, petrol (or gasoline) expands and this means you get less for your money. Ideally, fill up when the tank is half-full and fill the tank as slowly as possible.

- **Park in the shade**: On hot days, the obvious thing to do is park the car in the shade and use a windscreen shade. This saves on using the air-conditioning to cool the car when you return.

- **Keep coins in the car**: Always have some spare coins in the car ready to feed parking meters. This ultimately saves you a heart attack after viewing the parking ticket or wasting petrol driving around and around (and around) searching for a free car space.

- **Learn the tax rules**: Talk to your accountant or read the tax rules yourself to understand what types of trips qualify for a tax deduction. If you qualify, then make sure you keep the correct travel records in case you are audited.

5.6 Communication

Once upon a time, many years ago – actually less than 20 years ago – people astoundingly managed to survive without mobile phones. They would even go places and not be in contact with friends and family for hours. They would make long car or bus journeys and do quaint things like read a book or look out the window and day dream. They would also be known to write letters and send them off in the mail.

Gone are those days it seems. Now it seems that nobody goes anywhere without some sort of mobile device and all of this constant, frenetic communication is costing them big money. Follow these tips to trim your communication budget:

- **Ditch the land line:** If you and your family virtually sleep with your mobile phone and rarely use a landline, then why have still got one? Unless it's a 'free' inclusion in your plan, then it's time to ditch this technological relic.

- **Shop around:** Again, don't automatically renew any mobile phone or internet plan without shopping around in the market for a better deal. Contact at least three competitors to find out how flexible they are with their pricing and play one off against the other to get a cheaper price.

- **Pay as you go:** What better way to naturally restrict your usage than to get on a plan where you are forced to pay each month but can quit the plan at any time. If times are tough, you want flexibility in all the financial contracts you have signed.

- **Review your communication needs**: How do you know if you are on the best plan unless you step back and analyse when and where you are making calls or using the internet.

- **Good-bye mobile phone & internet**: It was so nice knowing you and the party seemed to be going along just fine – except of course when the bills came in. However, if you need to make a choice between putting food on the table or having constant access to Facebook, then make the right decision. Ditch them both. After about a week of withdrawal symptoms, you'll probably find that your life starts to change in many positive ways. You'll have more time for your children. More time to exercise. More time to have real conversations and of course, more time to work out a plan to get your finances back on track. Just don't replace an internet addiction with a television addiction! Oh, and remember that carrying a mobile phone is *not* needed to improve your security. In fact, mobile phones usually give people a false sense of security and they do things they shouldn't do – like take short cuts down dark alleys on their own. Think about it, the mobile phone is going to be rather useless if someone grabs you from behind and sticks a knife into your neck. You won't have time to say, 'Excuse me. I just need to call the police. Could you hold off attacking me until I've made the call?'

- **Avoid the post office:** The cost of posting even a standard sized letter is increasing each year. If it's possible for you to contact people by email using free internet at the library, then use this method as your preferred communication means. The savings will run into the thousands of dollars!

- **Meet people in real life:** With all this crazy social networking, it's time to down i-Phones or Androids and actually meet people for a real conversation. Remember – you won't die if you can't connect!

- **Cut international call costs**: Consider using Skype (www.skype.com) to make cheap internet calls and be VERY careful of international roaming costs!!

5.7 Clothes

5.7.1 Budget

You should never, *ever* pay full price for clothing. There are just too many opportunities to obtain clothes either for free or for greatly reduced prices. Here are 22 tips to reduce your clothing budget:

- **Find a friend:** This is where all that chatting outside the school gates with other parents starts to pay off – big time! If you can find a friend that has a child of the same sex but say around 2 year's older and that child is their youngest child of that sex, then you're onto a winner. Simply offer to save them a trip to the charity bins by taking any clothes (or toys) that their child has outgrown.

- **Use second hand (or thrift) shops:** It's utterly astounding what some people throw out. Remember what is one person's trash can very well be your treasure. Better yet, hunt down liquidation sales and negotiate hard for any item you buy.

- **Buy less clothes:** If you have cupboards bursting at the seams with clothes all over the place, then you are very likely a guilty shopper who goes on shopping binges without a care in the world for your bank balance. The 80/20 rule applies to many things in life but none more so than clothing where people typically wear 20% of their clothing at least 80% of the time.

- **Swap with friends:** If there are items in your cupboard that you haven't used for at least 12 months, the odds are high that it probably will never be worn. This is what is called a 'shopping blunder'. You can rectify it by finding a friend who is the same size and swapping it for something you really need.

- **Give useful gifts:** No doubt friends and family will want to shower your little offspring in gifts for their birthday or Christmas. Try to make them useful ones by communicating with everyone what clothes size they will be wearing next. Don't just assume that people will know their clothing size.

- **Online shopping:** Use eBay (www.ebay.com) or have a look at bulk discount websites such as:
  - Ezibuy (www.ezibuy.com.au)
  - 10 Dollar Mall (www.10dollarmall.com),
  - everything5pounds (www.everything5pounds.com),
  - Target (www.target.com.au),
  - Ozsale (www.ozsale.com.au)
  - Cocoalee (www.cocoalee.com.au).

- **Buy out of season or end of season:** At the end of summer, retailers know that people are not going to be buying summer clothes for at least another six to nine months. So, this is the time they will heavily discount those items to move them off the shelves.

- **Research the market price:** If you have access to the internet then use it and shop around at various stores to see just how cheaply you can get that favourite pair of jeans or dress that you have your heart set on.

- **Visit factory outlets or seconds stores:** Sometimes you can find a bargain or at least get an item that you really, really want for far less than the more expensive high street store. However, be careful about buying designer labels as you usually pay a premium just to walk around with their brand name all over your body. There is no good reason to be an unpaid, advertisement for them.

- **Get a store card:** As long as it's free to join and you will get benefits almost immediately, then it can sometimes be worthwhile getting a store card that provides discounts and special offers. Be warned though, if you need to make a purchase of at least $500 just to save $10 then the whole thing is a waste of your time.

- **Wait for the REAL sales:** These days many stores have perpetual sales which are a complete waste of your time. You don't want a 10% mark down in the price, you want a 50% (or greater) mark down. Even better is the 'closing down sale'! Also, remember that it's not a bargain if you never wear it.

- **Negotiate the price**: If you are at the markets, then it's entirely appropriate to ask if the vendor can offer you the item at a lower price. However, don't think you can't try this at a high street store either. In tough times, everything is negotiable.

- **Hire clothes**: If men can get away with hiring their suits for a wedding, then women can get away with hiring clothes such as their wedding dress or high school formal outfits.

- **Learn to sew**: Remember those painful sewing lessons at high school in home economics? If not, take the time to attend sewing classes. It could end up being one of your best investments. Not only will you have cheaper clothes, but you can also keep up with the latest fashions.

- **Buy classics**: Anything that is too trendy will be so 'last-year' within months. It will also have very limited re-use for future years. Avoid buying clothing that is too fashionable. Instead stick to classic wardrobe pieces that are timeless. For example, buying a pair of good quality jeans (at a discount price) is an item of clothing that should last you for at least 5 years or longer. Leather handbags are also a good choice as leather not only looks good, it should last decades.

- **Stick to a colour scheme**: Having a wardrobe of clothes that follow the same theme with compatible colours means you have more options to mix and match items.

- **Care for your clothes**: Common sense dictates that if you take care of your clothes, they will last a lot longer. If buttons fall off, then replace them immediately. Make sure you hang clothes up rather than leave them in an untidy heap on the floor. Read the label to ensure you follow the correct washing instructions and avoid washing them more than necessary. Try to buy items that don't require ironing or dry-cleaning. Make sure you change out of your work clothes immediately after you get home to keep them as fresh as possible.

- **Know your measurements:** Forget knowing your 'size' as every clothing manufacturer (and country) has a different sizing system. Instead get a tape measure out and measure your chest, waist and hips. Memorise these vital statistics or save them on a card in your wallet.

- **Buy for your current size**: Never, ever buy clothes thinking you'll diet to fit into them. Instead, buy those great new clothes as a reward after you've lost the weight. When you do lose weight, make sure you take the time to savour the moment and enjoy that hard-earned feeling of loose clothing around your hips and waistline.

- **Purchase iron-on patches**: If you have children – particularly boys – then iron-on patches for their pants will fit nicely over the holes that tend to form over the knee area.

- **Wear fake jewellery:** What is the point paying hundreds (or thousands) of dollars for the 'real thing'. Instead buy fake jewellery that doesn't need to be professionally cleaned or insured. Plus, it has the added benefit that if you end up accidently losing an earring down the shower drain (or toilet), it will not cost you a fortune in plumbing fees trying to retrieve it.

- **Use accessories wisely:** You may not need to go out and buy any new pieces at all if you are clever with buying accessories. A smart choice of scarf or new fake jewellery can change a look completely!

5.7.2 Stain Removal

To extend the life of your existing clothes, use this handy stain removal list:

#	Type of Stain	Remedy
1	Blood	Use cold water or ice on fresh blood stains. If the stain has dried use a 3% hydrogen peroxide solution.
2	Ink	Polyester - Use hair spray and allow it to dry on the stain before washing. Cotton – Apply rubbing alcohol and allow it to dry before washing normally.
3	Red wine	Blot the stain as quickly as possible and soak in cold water. Use a fabric stain remover and wash the item immediately.
4	Oil	Cover the entire stain in cornflour and leave overnight. Use a stain remover and wash in the hottest water the fabric will tolerate.
5	Grass	Pat the stain with a vinegar-soaked cloth or sponge. Apply a fabric stain remover and soak overnight. Rinse and wash normally.
6	Lipstick	Blot the stain with a cloth that has been soaked in rubbing alcohol.

#	Type of Stain	Remedy
7	Sweat or deodorant stains	Apply vinegar and then sprinkle salt on top of the stain. Leave for 30 minutes and then wash in hot, soapy water. If the stain still remains and the item is white cotton or polyester, try soaking the item in a diluted bleach solution overnight.
8	Tomato sauce, chocolate, coffee, red wine	Run lukewarm or cold water through the back of the stain immediately. Then gently rub a small amount of liquid detergent into the stain. Wash normally.
9	Mud / dirt	Soak in warm soapy water to remove as much of the dirt as possible. Apply a fabric stain remover and then wash normally.
10	Urine	Rinse the item immediately in warm water. Then soak the item in soapy water for at least 3-4 hours. Wash normally.
11	Chewing gum	Place the item into the freezer. Once the gum is hard it will be easy to scrape off.

- Your chances of successful stain removal diminish the longer the stain remains on a garment.

- Most clothing stains happen outside the home. In the absence of any other alternative, treat stains immediately with a napkin or cloth soaked in water.

- Never rub a stain. Instead pat or dab it with a cloth to avoid spreading it to a larger area.

- Always treat stains before putting clothes into the washing machine.

- Stain remover should always be applied to the back of the stain so it drives the stain away from the surface and not further into the garment.

5.8 Entertainment

The best things in life are usually free and this also applies to entertaining. Here, you can make very big savings with very little effort. In fact, you can cut the budget to zero as entertainment is a 'want' rather than a 'need' and in tough times you have to focus on needs rather than wants.

5.8.1 Holidays

- **Cancel vacations:** It doesn't take a genius to work this out but if you don't have the money then don't take a holiday. It couldn't be simpler.

- **Hunt down free activities**: On public holidays, most city councils hold free concerts and activities. Make the most of them – particularly any free meals that may accompany the event.

- **Have a staycation**: Why go to all the effort of paying for airline tickets and accommodation costs when you could stay at home and holiday in your own city? Pretend you are a tourist and see all the museums and public attractions that you've probably never seen before because you thought you could see it anytime – but never got around to it. Now is your big chance!

- **Swap houses:** If you have friends or relatives living in another city, why not arrange to swap houses and cars for the holidays. Just remember to check out insurance policies beforehand – particularly if you have a different driver for your car.

- **Travel in the off season:** Always try to avoid school holidays and peak season (which is summer time and religious holidays such as Christmas and Easter). Often the early months of autumn or late months of spring still have pretty good weather. An added bonus is there will be fewer crowds at popular tourist attractions.

- **Pack light:** With airlines constantly looking for new ways to charge passengers, make sure you pack as little as possible to avoid paying hefty airline luggage fees. Avoid taking valuables on any trip and always pack anything expensive or breakable in your hand luggage.

- **Avoid weekends**: Almost everything to do with entertainment, is more costly and crowded on a weekend. If possible, travel or attend events during the week.

- **Shop around for better deals:** Always check the price of competing airline tickets on the internet to see if you can get flights at a cheaper rate.

- **Try for last minute offers:** Get online and see what airlines, hotels, restaurants etc. are offering in terms of last-minute specials. In Australia, check out Wotif (www.wotif.com) or LastMinute (www.lastminute.com.au). There are sure to be similar offerings in other countries. Remember that two one-way tickets may actually be cheaper as you are not forced to travel both flights with the same airline.

- **Book early:** Sometimes the early bird does get the worm! Airline tickets can often be significantly cheaper if you buy them well in advance of travelling.

- **Look for courier flights:** If you are flexible with dates, then consider travelling as a courier in order to get either a free or heavily discounted ticket. Check out the website www.courierlist.com for further information.

- **Travel overnight:** A great way to save on accommodation costs is to travel overnight on planes, trains and boats. This will also maximise the time you can spend at your final destination. It is also a good plan if you are travelling with small children.

- **Always buy travel insurance:** It's a well-known cliché, but if you can't afford insurance, then you can't afford to travel. This applies particularly to international travel where medical expenses could cripple you financially if there was any sort of accident or problem with your travel plans.

- **Check your credit card insurance:** Many credit cards automatically include travel and/or car rental insurance when you use them to make travel bookings. Make sure you read the fine print or phone them before paying for additional insurance that you don't need.

- **Make a holiday budget:** Research costs on the internet and contact tourist information centres to get a good idea of the prices for various activities and accommodation. Work out the big spending items *before* leaving home. Try and be as flexible as possible with both the time and place for all activities you are planning.

- **Ask for a discount:** If you are booking directly with a hotel, remember to use your negotiating skills. Always ask them, 'Is that the best price I can do for that room?' Alternatively, say something like "Can you offer me a discount on that rate?" If a discount isn't possible, then maybe a free room upgrade might swing the deal? Always keep things pleasant. Never, ever get angry as this will rapidly increase your chances of getting a room right next to a noisy elevator. Remember, sometimes it works and sometimes it doesn't, but you'll never know if you never give it a go!

- **Ask for an upgrade:** Get the nicest person in your travelling group to smile sweetly and ask if it's possible for a free upgrade. Every once in a while, the universe responds and you can get lucky!! But you will never get an upgrade if you don't even ask!!

- **Buy experiences**: Most souvenirs will eventually be thrown out or contribute to clutter in your home. Put the money towards experiences rather than materialism. For example, take a tour rather than buy t-shirts or stuffed fluffy toys that end up creating clutter that is eventually thrown out.

- **Working holiday**: If you plan to travel around Europe or the USA, consider working to help pay for your holiday costs. Look out for farm stays, youth camps (Camp America) or even a Kibbutz in Israel.

- **Stay in hostels**: Pass up the sterile hotel room where you never get the chance to meet people and stay at a youth (or backpackers) hostel for a fraction of the price. There are usually no upper age restrictions and many offer single or family rooms along with shared accommodation.

- **Hide things well**: Nothing ruins a holiday at the beach faster than stolen money or jewellery. Outsmart petty criminals by cleaning out an old bottle of shampoo or sunscreen that has a wide opening and use it to hide precious items.

- **Leave expensive items at HOME**: Unless you are travelling to a very wealthy country, don't take any items which are expensive or have sentimental value. Grandma's pearl earrings or a 21st birthday watch or ring are best left safely at home. Showing off expensive stuff sends out a message saying "Please rob me as I'm a gullible tourist."

5.8.2 Children

- **Visit local parks:** Kids and adults need to get outside for fresh air and exercise. Why pay for it at expensive indoor entertainment venues? Instead, discover your local park and use the swings etc. If they are in derelict condition, contact your council to see what can be done to improve them.

- **Go to the library:** Lots of libraries have weekly activities and storytelling for young children. Plus, the DVDs and books are all free to borrow. Just remember to avoid fines by returning them on time.

- **Join a toy library**: It might take some hunting down, but a toy library could well end up being your biggest source of savings. It also gives you a brilliant opportunity to try out a toy before you buy it.

- **Board games:** On a cold, wet Sunday afternoon, nothing beats playing Monopoly on the floor of the lounge room. Throw in the smell of a roast dinner cooking in the oven and you have a very happy family activity.

- **Try new transport:** If your children rarely travel by anything other than a car, then a boat, bus or train trip can be a very exciting adventure for them - even if the destination is not particularly exciting (for the parents).

- **Visit local museums**: In many places, museums have free entry. This gives you an opportunity to expand your own knowledge and educate your children. A perfect entertainment venue for frugal, budget-conscious families.

- **Join a play group:** These are usually held in council or church halls and are a brilliant way of meeting other parents of young children. Plus, they usually have really good toys and activities for the kids.

- **Go camping:** Children are drawn to the great outdoors and you will bond as a family under that canvas tent. Even more so if the weather is inclement and you spend the entire trip inside the tent. Camping is a great way to have a family holiday on a tight budget. Look out for National Parks with their bargain basement fees.

- **Delay bigger holidays:** If your youngest child is less than 5 year's old, delay spending money on expensive overseas holidays or resort style accommodation. Not only will they be unable to appreciate the experience, they are also unlikely to even remember it.

- **Save cardboard boxes:** Don't throw out cereal boxes or toilet rolls as kids will have hours of entertainment cutting them up creating new things. Store them in a special "craft cupboard" and bring them out on rainy days.

- **Buy multi-purpose toys:** Avoid buying toys that only have one function. Instead toys like building blocks or painting kits can be used again and again in different ways. This means kids are unlikely to get bored with them as they can always use their imagination to create something different.

- **Cook with the kids:** Teach young children how to make simple patty cakes and biscuits. It's a great way to entertain them for at least an hour and they learn important new cooking and maths skills.

- **Visit the airport:** For the price of a bus or train ticket, bundle up the kids and make a day out of going to the airport and watching the planes take off and land. Kids are often entertained by the simplest things and getting on a bus or watching a plane land is an exciting event.

- **Leave after lunch:** If you are heading out with kids to the beach or to the park, make sure you leave after filling them up on breakfast or lunch. Make sure you take plenty of snacks to avoid the need to buy expensive take-away foods.

- **Avoid buying activity books:** Don't waste money buying expensive activity and colouring books that are never used. Instead print off activity sheets from the internet. Check out these websites:
  - Sesame Street (www.sesamestreet.org)
  - BBC CBeebies (www.bbc.co.uk/children)
  - The Wiggles (www.thewiggles.com.au)
  - ABC4Kids (www.abc.net.au/abcforkids).

- **Make your own play dough:** Get your kids to help make the dough and then store it in an air-tight container to be used again and again for up to 6 months.
  - Ingredients: ½ cup salt, 1 tablespoon oil, 1 cup plain flour, 1 cup water, 1 tablespoon cream of tartar, food colouring.
  - Method: Mix all the ingredients in a saucepan and stir over a low heat until it forms a dough texture. Store the mixture in a sealed container in the fridge.

5.8.3 Birthdays

- **Simple, useful gifts:** The ideal gift for a birthday is something that will be useful to the recipient and inexpensive for the person buying it. Items that fit this requirement include: coffee mugs, stationery, plants, seeds, pots, candles, soap, homemade biscuits or jam.

- **Bake a cake:** Find out the recipient's favourite type of cake. Then go off and create a masterpiece by making full use of decorative icing to personalise the results.

- **Gift cards:** If you don't have any idea what to give someone then consider buying them a gift card. This means the recipient can go out and buy something they really need.

- **Offer a service:** Instead of offering a material gift, offer a service. For example, offer to mow lawns, tidy the house for a month, clean windows, cars etc.

- **Handpicked flowers:** As a thoughtful gesture, head to the garden and pick some flowers. Tie a ribbon around the stems and present them as a lovely birthday gift.

- **Re-gifting**: At some point in your life you will get a gift that you know that you will never, ever use. However, all is not wasted as that unwanted gift can be re-gifted. Just make sure that the new recipient will never, ever meet up with the original gift giver.

- **Buy / sell on E-Bay**: The alternative to re-gifting is selling the item. This can be online via websites such as E-Bay or through a garage sale. The flip side is that these places can also be a great source of cheaper gifts for your own family and friends.

- **Make your own gift cards**: Never, ever buy an expensive greeting card when you can make it yourself. The internet is awash with great ideas for making personalised cards.

- **Write a poem:** A beautiful hand-made card with a simple poem especially written for the recipient will be remembered and treasured forever.

- **Head off to the movies:** This plan works best for a smaller group of 3 or 4 people. Skip the cake and you only need to pay for the movie tickets, popcorn and drinks.

- **Send invitations via email:** Not only will you save paper, cartridge toner, envelopes and stamps but you will also save time as you can send out one snazzy email invitation to everyone at the same time! This also has the advantage of letting everyone know who has been invited to the party.

- **Party in the park:** Using a local park for a party automatically reduces the venue costs to ZERO! The swings, toilets and tables are also free - plus sometimes there are also free barbeques available. Grab some pizzas, drinks and a home-made cake to complete the perfect birthday party.

- **Combine parties:** If you have two children (or two friends) born around the same time of year, then pick a date that is mid-way between both birthdays and celebrate the event together. This works especially well if relatives have to travel long distances to attend parties for both people.

5.8.4 Christmas

- **Hold a secret Santa:** This works particularly well in large families or offices. Get each person to write their name and three desired gifts on a small piece of paper and put the paper into a hat or box. Make sure people are told to list gifts under a specified price limit. Then draw two names out of the hat. Those people will buy gifts for each other. Continue until there are no names left. If there are three names left, then each person has to buy two presents, however they will be rewarded by getting two presents themselves. Not only does this method save people buying large numbers of gifts, but it also ensures people receive things that they really want.

- **Send email cards**: There are many websites such BlueMountain (www.bluemountain.com), Hallmark (www.hallmark.com) or 123 Greetings (www.123.greetings.com) that let you send out beautiful free email cards at Christmas.

- **Save wrapping & cards:** If you are given gifts with beautiful wrapping or cards, reuse them for birthday parties or Christmas gifts.

- **Offer IOUs:** When money is really tight, print out simple cards with personalised messages offering a service, for example: "Merry Christmas. This card can be exchanged for ONE clean of your car."

- **Make home-made gifts**: Get the kids involved in making home-made gifts for family members at Christmas. Bookmarks with photos of the children are always a simple but thoughtful gift. Alternatively, fill up a clean, glass coffee or jam jar with chocolates and lollies. Tie a colourful ribbon around the outside and presto – you have another cheap (but thoughtful) Christmas gift.

- **Buy decorations after Christmas**: Get ready for the next Christmas holiday season by shopping the day after Christmas when everything is massively discounted. Stores have to pay money to remove stock that can't sit out on display during the year and so they would much rather customers buy it instead. To encourage sales and to let you know how serious they are about it, prices are often cut by 75% or more on Christmas items.

- **Buy gifts after Christmas**: Retailers are highly motivated to clear floor stock after the big Christmas sales have passed. They know that many items will sit there unsold for months (if not longer) and this is costing them money. Try and arrange to meet family and friends after Christmas and thereby delay buying their gifts until they are discounted. In many cities, the post-Christmas sales are legendary. Don't waste this opportunity to make big savings!

- **Be flexible with traditions:** Quite simply, there is no law that says you have to give gifts on the 25th December. Instead it might make a lot of sense to attend Christmas carols and/or church services on the 25th December but wait until the post-Christmas sales to exchange gifts. Similarly, there is no law about serving turkey when cheaper cuts of meat (or even none) may be more affordable.

- **Stock up on snacks:** To avoid a massive grocery shopping bill in December, add a few non-perishable items to your trolley each week over October and November.

- **Buy useful gifts:** Kids always need new clothes or stationery for school so make them part of their Christmas stocking!

Golden Tip: If your budget is really tight, then don't make things even tighter for yourself by overspending at Christmas. Agree to only buy presents for the children and give yourself the gift of less worry about money.

5.8.5 Weddings

There is probably no greater sign of financial insanity than to go into debt at the start of a marriage. In fact, it's almost a sure-fire way to end up divorced. Obviously, every couple and their families will have preconceived ideas about the type of wedding they want to hold. However, under no circumstances should a couple be forced into debt to appease religious, cultural or family expectations. Easier said than done, but if it's not possible to avoid a large wedding itself, at least there are ways to cut down on a large wedding bill.

- **Get organised:** Download a free, simple wedding planner from A Practical Wedding (www.apracticalwedding.com) and set up a detailed budget, guest list, vendor contact list and timeline for the event.

- **Research, research, research:** Many people don't have a clue what they want for their big day. Check out websites such as Martha Stewart Weddings (www.marthastewartweddings.com) or The Knot (www.theknot.com.au) to get inspiration.

- **Marry in the off-season:** Just as you should travel in the off-season, you should also consider marrying in the off-season. As most weddings are held in late spring or summer, you will inevitably have more options in winter or autumn. Remember that it can often be a lot cheaper to get married on a week day rather than Saturday or Sunday.

- **Slash the catering budget:** One of the biggest costs is catering. You can save a small fortune by holding a lunch-time wedding which obviously will have a lot less alcohol. It may be an even better idea to hold a mid-morning wedding (say 10 am). This means you only need to serve your guests light refreshments and can serve guests a token glass of champagne for the toast.

- **Make the wedding cake**: Use your web browser to search for information on "homemade wedding cakes". Remember to have a trial run to make sure you can actually make the cake correctly. Keep the design as simple as possible and use ribbons, flowers or pre-made iced decorations.

- **Rent all the clothes**: Never, ever buy clothing that will only be worn once. Rent or borrow the wedding dress and any other special clothing worn by the bridal party. Keep the number of attendants down to a small, manageable number.

- **Skip the 'wedding' dress:** If you can't find the right wedding dress to rent, simply buy a bridesmaid's dress that you can wear again for other functions. There is no rule that says you must wear a white expensive dress. Alternatively go to the websites which sell second hand wedding dresses such as: Pre-owned Wedding Dresses (www.preownweddingdresses.com).

- **Use flowers in season:** Keep the flowers to a minimum but always ensure the bride has the most beautiful bouquet you can afford. Tulips, gerberas or roses are always a lovely choice.

- **Prune the guest list**: This will be the hardest part of the entire wedding. One way to get around it is to invite people to come to the wedding itself and provide them with morning tea or brunch afterwards. If a main reception is absolutely necessary then reserve the bigger event for family members only and communicate this to all guests.

- **Delay the honeymoon**: Why bundle all the fun into just one short period of your life? Instead, schedule a holiday for a special anniversary or before you are expecting a baby.

- **Wedding invitations:** Now you have cut the guest list to an inch of its life, there should be a lot less invitations to write. Use some of your creative genius to make handmade invitations. Visit the website Meridian Bride (www.meridianbride.com) for further inspiration.

- **Get family to pay**: If your parents are insisting upon 250 guests to attend the reception, then diplomatically say that your budget doesn't stretch that far but they are more than welcome to invite all these people if they agree to pay for them. It's amazing how guest lists rapidly reduce in numbers once this has been decided. Besides it used to be the tradition that the parents paid for most of the wedding anyway.

- **DIY – Hair, Makeup and Nails**: You should already have a very simple hair style (to save money on grooming) so expensive hairdressing on your wedding day should not be needed. Similarly, doing your makeup and nails are skills you can easily pickup from YouTube (www.youtube.com) videos. If you are desperate, arrange for a friend to do it for you or get free lessons via an in-store makeup trial done by department store staff.

- **Skip the engagement ring**: This is yet another item of jewellery that is expensive, rarely worn and needs to be insured. Instead of buying an engagement ring, put the money into buying two simple platinum or gold wedding bands. They will then be worn every day of your life.

- **Don't say the word 'wedding'**: As soon as you utter this sacred word you are doomed to pay the highest possible price a vendor will charge. Instead say something like, 'family reunion' or 'party' and then get the quote for their services.

- **Select a cheaper venue**: Consider getting married in a local park with a pretty pond or rotunda. Alternatively, use a university campus, beach, historic site or museum. Remember to check to see if permits are required beforehand.

- **Prune your photographic dreams**: Another massive expense is photography. Don't fall for the 250-photo package offered by many 'artistic photographers', thinking that you need that many photos to capture the event. In truth, you only need about 10-20 good quality photos at key moments throughout the ceremony. Get the best couple of photos made up into larger prints and framed, then give them as gifts to your parents. Keep a few for yourself and have the rest of them placed into a special photo album.

- **Shop around for music:** Hire a string quartet from your local music school and get them to play throughout the reception. This should work out a lot cheaper (and quieter) than hiring a band. Plus, it will bring an element of ambience and sophistication to the event.

- **Make your own decorations:** To reduce the cost of a reception, use your creativity and the internet to come up with DIY decorations.

- **Elope:** When it all gets too hard, simply pack your bags, go off on a holiday and elope while you are away. Nothing could be simpler – although it may take years to repair the emotional damage if your parents were dead set on a traditional church wedding with hundreds of guests.

- **Use a registry office**: One way to avoid the trauma of eloping is to invite friends and family out for a formal lunch (where they think you are about to announce your engagement). Before you go in to eat, pop into the registry office and get married. Then afterwards celebrate with them at the restaurant. It will certainly be a wedding that nobody will ever forget!

5.8.6 Other

- **Research, research, research**: If you are planning any sort of holiday or entertainment activity, always check up on the internet to see if there are cheaper options.

- **Don't buy new books or magazines:** Instead borrow them from the library or from friends. If you absolutely must have a new release, buy a pre-loved version on eBay or from a second hand store.

- **Ditch pay television**: Remember that you will not die if you can't watch the grand final of the cricket, football or any other sport. Cancel your pay television subscription and find a friend who does have access to it. As a courtesy gesture, make sure you bring the pizza or drinks.

- **Bring a plate (pot luck)**: If friends or family are coming around to your home for a get-together, ask people to bring a plate of food with them. To avoid everyone turning up with the same thing, suggest in your invitation whether they bring sweet or savoury foods.

- **Free lectures and films:** Take advantage of any free lectures or tutorials at local colleges and universities.

- **Buy a season pass**: Many sports offer substantial discounts if you buy a season pass to see all their matches versus pay-as-you-go arrangements.

- **Attend a matinee performance:** Usually concerts are cheaper if held during the week or at lunch time. Always try to be flexible with timing to make big savings on your entertainment budget.

- **Make use of happy hour:** If a bar or restaurant is offering free food or drinks for an hour or so - then make good use of it. Free food is never something to be refused but remember to drink alcohol responsibly.

- **Share costs with friends**: The more people you have sharing a room or hire car, the cheaper the overall cost will be for each person. It can also give you more bargaining power to obtain a hotel discount.

- **Save used toiletries from hotels:** If you have opened any of the toiletries in a hotel, then don't leave them behind afterwards. Anything opened will be thrown out by the cleaners. Instead, take it with you and use it at home. Keep any empty containers as they can be re-used when going on short breaks or for school camps.

- **Find kids' specials:** Many restaurants or movie theatres have special nights where kids can eat free or at a reduced cost. Usually Tuesday nights tend to be the slowest for many entertainment venues, so they try to boost sales by making enticing offers.

- **Substitute items**: Use your imagination to save money by substituting one expensive activity for a much cheaper version. For example, instead of staying in a hotel, borrow camping equipment and sleep in a tent or instead of eating at a restaurant, pack a picnic basket and head off to the beach.

5.9 Education

5.9.1 General

- **Buy second hand textbooks:** Find a student who is in the year ahead, to buy cheap textbooks. Alternatively, use copies in the library – although they will always be highly sought after by other smart students doing the same thing. For an even cheaper alternative, share pre-loved textbooks with fellow students or look out for digital versions that you can rent.

- **Use home stationery:** Check what supplies you already have at home before going out to buy new scissors, pencils etc. Most of these items are good to use year after year. Plan things wisely and you won't end up with a stationery cupboard filled with scissors that are never used.

- **Buy in bulk**: Where it makes sense, try and buy items frequently used items such as pencils, paper and colouring pens in bulk. This prevents the need to go out shopping again throughout the school year.

- **Wait for the sales**: There are bargains aplenty during the back-to-school sales. Hold off buying anything new until those ubiquitous catalogues start appearing in the mailbox.

5.9.2 Primary and Secondary Education

- **Justify private education**: There can be many benefits for children that attend a private school. However, ask yourself whether it's possible to get those same benefits at a much cheaper price. Perhaps moving to a better suburb or city and attending a local government or selective school will allow your children to get just as good an education as they would have received at an expensive private school. Plus, savings made on fees could easily go to extra-curricular activities like piano lessons, ballet classes etc. Just remember, if you do take the private education path, justify exactly what you are paying for and question whether you really are getting good value for your money.

- **Start university or college early:** If your child has high enough grades and the opportunity is available, then strongly consider taking early tertiary education courses. These are often heavily discounted in price. Plus, they usually have the added bonus of additional entrance points if the course is successfully completed.

- **Use the clothing pool**: Almost every school that requires students to wear a uniform will have a clothing pool or second-hand shop. Use it! The money spent often goes to school fundraising and you can get a big discount on clothing and other items.

- **Label EVERYTHING**: Unless you like the idea of having all your clever, cost-cutting activities undone, get out the permanent marker and label everything with your child's name. Items that are typically lost include: hats, jumpers, lunch boxes, books, water bottles – basically, everything your child takes to school.

- **Prevent head lice & worms**: Avoid the need to go out and buy expensive head lice treatment or worm tablets by taking steps to prevent them in the first place. Encourage your children to wash their hands regularly and always before eating food. Keep hair as short as possible and for girls it must be tied back in pigtails or a braid.

- **Share care with other parents**: During holidays or even school term, do a deal with another parent (or parents) to care for their child one afternoon a week in return for the same favour. It will save everyone a fortune on childcare costs.

- **Break in new shoes:** To prevent blisters in the first week of school, always get break in new shoes the week before school starts. This can easily be done by wearing them for a couple of hours each day.

5.9.3 Tertiary Education

- **Apply for scholarships**: If it doesn't cost you any money to apply, then it's foolhardy not to throw your hat into the ring and apply for a tertiary education scholarship.

- **Get your employer to pay**: Many large employers and public service roles (particularly at universities) allow employees to complete self-education courses related to their work and pay the course fees on successful completion.

- **Look for free courses:** An increasing number of universities now offer free online (or taster) courses that give students credit if they continue on with the programme. What better way to find out whether a course is the right one for you than to 'try before you buy'? It can also give you a massive head start on your fellow students. Look at Openculture (www.openculture.com), KhanAcademy (www.khanacademy.org) or University of the People (www.uopeople.org) for inspiration.

- **Graduate on time (or earlier)**: One of the best ways of cutting education expenses is to avoid failing exams or changing courses. Both situations can be prevented by careful planning. Firstly, study hard to avoid needlessly failing courses. Secondly, get as much work experience as possible in the area in which you want to study before you even set foot inside a lecture theatre.

- **Get a part-time job**: No matter how busy your schedule, if you are studying full-time you can still squeeze in some sort of part-time job. Even if it needs to be in the holidays, a part-time job will give you skills and experience that no university or college education can ever match. Plus, it comes with important benefits – money! Be even smarter and try and get a part-time job in the same area as you plan to work full-time.

- **Consider live-in, home-help:** Many elderly people loathe the thought of moving into a retirement village but are living in a home too large for their current needs. A compromise for them could be if a (quiet) student moved into one of the spare rooms and in return for free rent and meals, they do all the shopping and home maintenance tasks for the elderly person. This creates a win-win situation. The only catch is that you wouldn't be able to bring home friends for any loud, student parties.

- **Reconsider tertiary study:** If you don't have any idea whatsoever what you want to do with your life, then don't waste precious time and money sitting in pointless university lectures and scraping through courses with low grade pass marks. Get out in the world and learn through experience what really interests you. Then keep your job (plus income) and study by distance education to complete your degree or diploma.

5.10 Financial Services

It's a jungle out there and the predators are lurking in banks and insurance companies waiting for their prey. They lure you in to buying their products and services like a Greek siren, only to have you face the same fate (financially) as the poor sailors subjected to their alluring voices. Nowhere is the potential to be ripped off higher than in the financial services sector. <u>You have been warned!</u>

Soppy television and print advertising spins a story that your local bank is on your side. Nothing could be further from the truth. These people are in business. Whether it's selling you a mortgage, personal loan, insurance, managed fund or superannuation (pension) solutions, make no mistake - they are not a charity – they are in the game to make money.

5.10.1 Insurance

- **Query insurance renewal notices**: Just like car insurance renewal notices, never accept a renewal notice for life, health or home insurance without shopping around for a better deal. The internet has a great source of comparison websites and often it's cheaper to buy the policy online.

Country	Sample Website(s) ***Remember to check the internet for even more websites.***
Australia	www.youi.com.au www.iselect.com.au www.canstar.com.au
New Zealand	www.interest.co.nz nz.sharpestquote.com
United Kingdom	www.moneysupermarket.com www.comparethemarket.com
USA / Canada	www.insurance.com www.kanetix.ca www.ehealthinsurance.com

- **Bundle insurances:** When getting a quote for insurance, tell the salesperson that you are willing to bundle other insurance policies to get a better deal. So, for example, if you are phoning for a quote on car insurance, ask them to also give a price for any other additional insurance you may have. Once you are given a quote, ask them "Is there any other way I can reduce the premium?"

- **Avoid extended warranties:** Most electrical goods are already sold with an existing manufacturer's warranty. Think twice about paying for extra insurance on whitegoods and electronic equipment. If the original warranty is for 12 months, ask yourself what are the chances the item is suddenly going to fail at 13 months? How many people do you know who have claimed on an extended warranty policy? Most likely no one! Remember that there are already existing laws to protect consumers. Don't just accept the extended warranty sales pitch but instead think it through. Is it *really* worth it, bearing in mind insurance companies will find a way to wriggle out of many policy payouts?

- **Increase insurance excess (deductibles):** The 'excess' is the payment you are willing to make out of your own money before an insurance company pays out any of their money. The greater the excess you agree to at the time the policy is written, the lower the insurance premiums. This can work well to reduce your payments but you need to make sure that you can afford to pay any excess in the event of a claim.
- **Find out risk reduction criteria:** Ask your insurance company what you can do to reduce costs. It could be as simple as installing a car alarm to significantly reduce premiums.

5.10.2 Banking

- **Understand compound interest**: Einstein is quoted as saying "Compound interest is the eighth wonder of the world. He who understands it, earns it and he who doesn't, pays it." In simplified terms, this means you earn interest on top of the interest you have already earned and as time goes by the process accelerates.

- **Consider pre-paying annually**: This is where a calculator needs to come out. If the discount for paying bills annually is more than the interest you would receive by holding the money in a bank account (and allowing for taxation on this interest), then by all means – pay the bill annually. Otherwise, pay the bill around 3-4 days before it is due and not a second earlier. Time is money and the more time that money spends in your high interest bank account, the better.

- **Shop around to avoid bank fees**: Almost everything is negotiable in banking. If you don't want to pay ridiculous account keeping fees or ATM access fees, then shop around to find a financial service provider that does meet your needs. These banking giants make billions in profits. They truly can afford to stop rorting your bank accounts and you must stop them by voting with your feet.

- **Be cautious of high interest rates**: Often smaller or less credit worthy financial service providers will advertise interest rates higher than the banks. Be warned as the higher rate is usually to compensate for a greater risk to your capital.

- **Lock up your money:** Often the biggest obstacle in budgeting is impulse spending. To counteract the threat, make it harder for yourself by locking up your money in a term deposit or internet savings account.

- **Use own bank ATMs**: Plan your cash requirements so you don't need to use another bank's automatic teller machines (ATM) and incur high fees for the privilege.

- **Update your personal details**: It is highly likely that your name and details are regularly used by the bank for marketing purposes. That means your mail box is regularly targeted with amazing deals that are hard to ignore. Put a stop to temptation by phoning your bank and requesting to be placed on the 'Not for Marketing' list.

5.10.3 Mortgages

- **Ask for a rate reduction:** Times are tough in the mortgage business as more people default and less people buy properties. However, that shouldn't stop you for asking for a discount on your current mortgage rate, personal loan or even your credit card! Remember, nothing ventured - nothing gained!

- **Arrange a mortgage holiday:** If you have lost your job but think it will only be temporary and want to avoid the trauma of a mortgagee sale, try and negotiate a temporary suspension in repayments. Use this time wisely by springing into action by either finding another job or selling up. You are almost always guaranteed to get a better price for your home if you try and sell it before the bank.

- **Beware teaser mortgage rates:** Banks and other financial institutions often use teaser rates to attract new customers. They offer people a very low mortgage rate for their first six or twelve months and then it reverts to a much higher rate afterwards. That new rate can often be a lot higher than the average rate of other financial institutions. Teaser rates may be a great deal if you can pay back the loan quickly. If not, then tread carefully and read the fine print of any documentation.

5.10.4 Credit Cards & Loans

- **Chop up credit cards:** If you are unable to pay off your credit card each month and thereby incur ridiculous, outrageously high interest rates then you are not in command of your own destiny and the credit card(s) have to go. Use scissors to slice them up into tiny little pieces. Remember to cancel the account with your financial service provider as soon as the balance is repaid.

- **Carry cards & cash:** Many retailers are now asking customers to pay a surcharge if they use a credit card. Make sure you have alternative cash sources at the ready to avoid surcharges.

- **Milk credit cards:** Alternatively, if you are self-disciplined with money and can pay back your credit card in full each month, then only pay the full amount owing a couple of days before it is due and get an interest free loan from the bank. The bank still makes money out of you as they charge the retailer a fee for processing their payment via a credit card. However, the bank makes nothing from you in interest and that's the way smart people should always use credit cards.

- **Get out of debt:** We talk about people being 'free' in western societies but you are not really free if you have a massive debt hanging over your head. Sort your life out so you can place a laser focus on getting out of debt as quickly as possible. Remember to pay off the debts with the highest interest rate first and usually this is found on credit cards.

- **Avoid lending money:** Shakespeare in Hamlet Act 1 obviously understood money with the words:

  > "Neither a borrow nor lender be
  > For loan oft loses both itself and friend,
  > And borrowing dulls the edge of husbandry."

- **Watch out for hidden fees:** The banks have a vested interest in keeping you in debt for as long as possible and extracting as much money out of you during that time. They do this via high interest rates and fees or charges. Often, they have penalties for early payouts on loans. Make sure you read the fine print on every loan or credit card contract. Remember that fees are **always** negotiable. If a bank wants your business enough, they can eliminate the fees or offer you some other sweetening deal.

- **Beware balance transfer cards**: If you have significant credit card debt, it may be highly tempting to sign up for a balance transfer card offering an enticing 0% interest rate for six months. This could potentially be a saviour for your finances if you are sensible and use the six months to get yourself out of debt. However, it's far more likely that you will end up using this six-month period to add further to the debt. Be very, very cautious about these types of offers. Banks are not in the charity business. They only offer these types of products because they know that most people are unable to pay back the full amount in a short period of time. After the six months has passed and the interest rate increases, they have another gullible customer paying lots of high interest payments.

- **Debt consolidation:** Depending on your circumstances, it may be sensible to consolidate your debts into one loan. This applies in particular when you have large credit card (high interest) debts which could be rolled into one (low interest) personal loan – or even added to a mortgage.

- **Check each statement:** Bank fraud is far more common than people realise. So, it is vital that you always review each monthly statement carefully to ensure every single item is accounted for in your budget.

5.11 Health

Don't you find it amazing that the media rarely discusses the most common forms of dying? It's like it never happens and when it does, people use euphemisms like "passed away" or "resting peacefully". It all fits in with this enormous taboo people seem to have with the D-word. Yet death is a fact of life and if more people knew the real statistics, they would be far more likely to pay serious attention to their health.

The main causes of death in western society include: heart disease, cancer, chronic lung disease, stroke, accidents, dementia, diabetes, kidney disease, influenza and suicide. So, doesn't it make sense to adopt a lifestyle that minimises your chances of getting these big killers?

- **Quit smoking:** If you smoke then you already know it is highly likely you'll die a horrible, painful and expensive death. However, before you depart this world for the next, think about the money you're literally blowing away. Cigarettes have a truck load of taxes attached to each packet making them an increasingly expensive habit. If the scary images now imprinted on every packet in Australia don't turn you off these cancer sticks, then the price should do it for you.

- **Avoid passive smoking:** If you quit smoking it reduces your risk of lung cancer and a whole host of other nasty, aggressive tumours. However, passive smoking is also a risk factor as you are still breathing in poisonous gases. Avoid places such as pubs or nightclubs where there are lots of people smoking. If you live with a smoker, make sure they do it outside and wait 5 minutes afterwards before coming inside to ensure that smoke has cleared from their lungs.

- **Limit alcohol:** Not only is it very expensive and high in calories, but it can also be highly addictive for many people. Yes, it can calm the nerves and give temporary relief from financial pressures but in the long run it won't solve anything and inevitably will make things much worse.

- **Eat healthy foods**: Avoid highly processed foods as these are most likely to have low nutritional content. Cut sugar and salt from your diet in order to reduce tooth decay and high blood pressure problems. Aim to eat at least 2 pieces of fruit and 3 different vegetables each day and only eat meat (of any kind) every other day.

- **Visit the dentist**: Brush your teeth at least twice a day and rinse your mouth regularly by drinking water. Dental floss must be used every evening to remove food caught between your teeth. Most dentists recommend visiting at least once every six months, but fees are now way beyond the budget of most families, so aim for a check-up once a year. If you live near a university or college that offers dental courses, phone them up to see if they treat members of the public for free or a reduced cost. Dentists always get free samples from tooth care companies, so remember to always ask for a free toothbrush and toothpaste at each visit.

- **Get regular health checks:** This applies particularly for the over 40's, but at least once a year have a health check done by your GP (medical doctor). They should check your blood pressure, eyesight, weight, skin (for cancer), diabetes etc. Remember to inform the doctor of any family history that could increase your own health risks.

- **Avoid kidney disease**: Protect your kidneys by drinking lots of water each day and avoiding salty foods (that increase your blood pressure). Maintain a sensible weight for your height and bone structure by exercising regularly for at least 30 minutes a day.

- **Prevent skin cancer**: Many years ago, in Australia there was a great television advertisement urging people to "slip on a shirt, slop on sunscreen and slap on a hat." It's also important to avoid the sun during the peak UV hours which are generally 10am - 3pm each day. Sunglasses should also be worn throughout the year to protect your eyes which are also easily damaged by the sun.

- **Drop gym memberships:** In tough times, you need to find another way to keep fit. This could be via mowing lawns (for money), delivering newspapers or pamphlets (for money), stacking shelves at a supermarket (for money). In other words, if you are moving and exercising your body, you may as well do it for money while you are young and have the energy levels! If you really feel that you need some sort of work out, borrow a fitness DVD from the library or watch the fitness television shows to get the same thing for free.

- **Health tourism:** There is now a thriving industry in India, South-East Asia and Eastern Europe where many medical and dental procedures can be done for a fraction of the cost charged in more developed countries. So, for example, if you require extensive dental work it might be worth your while checking the prices charged overseas and then combining the procedure with an overseas holiday to recuperate.

- **Strong social links:** Studies have shown that having strong social links increasing people's life expectancy. If you don't have family living nearby, it is even more important to get involved in community activities to build up a strong social network. Depending on how tough things get in the economy, these friendships may turn out to be life savers.

- **Re-think birth control:** If you have completed your family and are absolutely certain that you do not want any more children, consider permanent birth control. It will not only cost less but also completely remove the possibility of accidently conceiving a baby. Remember that the quickest and easiest way is for men to have a vasectomy. This is a simple, inexpensive 10-minute operation in a GP's surgery that does not require a general anaesthetic.

- **Keep track of expenses:** If there is any chance of a tax deduction for health expenses, then you need to keep copies of all scanned receipts and a detailed list of expenses.

5.11.1 Tips to Increase Exercise

Here are some great tips to squeeze fitness into a busy schedule:

- Turn your commute to school or work into exercise by walking or cycling. If it's not possible to go the entire distance, get off one station before your destination and walk the rest of the way.

- At work, take the stairs instead of the lift. Even if you catch the lift to level 30 and then walk up the stairs to level 40, you are getting some exercise into your day.

- Don't eat lunch at your desk. Instead get outside and take a brisk 15 - 30-minute walk. Arrange to do it with a friend so you have added motivation.

- Set your alarm 15 minutes earlier and go for a brisk walk around the block. Do the same thing in the evening.

- If you are waiting in a queue at the shops or even at the traffic lights, use that time as an opportunity to stretch your leg muscles or (for women) do pelvic floor exercises.

- While waiting for your children to complete their swimming or ballet lessons, don't just sit in the car. Use that time as an opportunity to either go swimming yourself or get out and do a quick walk.

5.11.2 Funerals

As distressing as funerals will always be, it is important to remember that funerals are for the living and not for the dead. The deceased (if they were alive) would likely turn in their grave at the massive amount of money being spent on their behalf. Funerals in Australia can cost anywhere from around $2,000 to $20,000 or more!

Remember there is no law that says you **must** use a funeral director. It's just an established tradition, much like people who think you need to hire a real estate agent to sell your home. The problem is that in the grip of grief, making any sort of decisions can be difficult if not impossible for most people. Funeral directors are aware of this fact and unfortunately some of them may exploit it by selling far more add-on features than people would have normally chosen. It's far better, to work out a funeral plan and budget well before you are close to the departure lounge. This also includes getting a Will prepared well in advance to save everyone time and money when your estate is finalised. If you have elderly relatives, talk to them discretely about their funeral plans and what they would like for their big send off. You are likely to be very surprised at how most people want very little spent from their estate on something that has limited value. Other savings include:

- **Use a crematorium:** Cremation is usually cheaper than burial because there is no casket required and a larger burial plot is not needed.

- **Have a graveside service**: If you know the deceased does not want to be cremated, hold a graveside service which will save on the cost of hiring rooms etc.

- **Avoid expensive services**: Hold a "no service cremation" and then schedule a memorial service or wake in your home.

- **Get three quotes**: If using a funeral director, get at least three quotes to ensure you are not being ripped off.

- **Skip advertising**: Inform all family and friends of the death by phone. Email or text messages are too impersonal. Remember that death notices in the newspapers are <u>not</u> compulsory.

- **Keep things simple**: Create an online memorial website (for free) rather than buying an expensive memorial headstone. People will be able to enter comments that you can print off later as a lasting memory.

- **Limit the flowers**: Just like engagement rings, flowers are a tradition but are certainly not a necessity at funerals. Instead of spending hundreds of dollars, buy one beautiful bouquet of flowers as a tasteful, symbolic gesture.

- **Slash the catering budget:** Another big cost is catering at the wake. Just like weddings, you can save a small fortune by holding it mid-morning or mid-afternoon. This means you will only need to serve your guests light refreshments.

- **Compassionate airfares:** Most major airlines offer discounted rates for people travelling to attend a funeral. It is always worth asking but make sure you do it at the time of booking!

5.12 Home Items

The frugal approach to buying home items is to have as few of them as you can possibly manage. Not only is an uncluttered home easier to keep tidy, it also means insurance costs will be cheaper. Here are 17 tips to keep costs to a minimum:

- **Buy second hand**: Things like child car seats and helmets are best bought new to ensure they meet the latest safety standards <u>and</u> do not carry damage from previous accidents rendering them unsafe. However, home items such as: desks, lamps, bed frames, tables etc. are best bought second hand. As soon as you buy any new furniture, it instantly loses value. Look out for garage or liquidation sales for some of the best bargains on offer. Alternatively, auctions (for deceased or bankrupt estates), pawn shops and charity stores are another great source of ultra-cheap furniture and electrical appliances.

  Make a few phone calls or send emails to real estate agents in your area asking if they have clients with excess furniture they want to offload. Many home sellers have items they don't want to take with them and this could be your big opportunity to get something for nothing! Look at websites such as:

Country	Sample Website(s) *Remember to check the internet for even more websites.*
Australia	www.totallyfreestuff.com, www.ozrecycle.com, www.freecycle.com.au, www.vinnies.org.au
New Zealand	www.freestuff.co.nz,
United Kingdom	www.frn.org.uk, www.recyleyourfurniture.co.uk, www.snaffleup.co.uk
USA	www.craigslist.org, www.fatwallet.com, www.pennysaverusa.com

- **Never buy the latest version**: For electrical goods, always be on the lookout for the previous year's version. If it is only a small step behind the latest version then save money by haggling for a lower price arguing that it is "not the latest version therefore nobody else will want it".

- **Haggle for a lower price:** When you buy a house or car, the advertised price is just the starting point for negotiating and something you should *always* avoid paying in full. Furniture and electrical goods are no different. Always ask for a discount before you buy anything and remember that it's okay to walk away from a potential sale. Alternatively, ask the store to price match if you have found the same item at another store for a cheaper price.

- **Pay with cash:** Retailers have to pay credit card companies a percentage of each sale. It can be anything around 2-3% of the purchase price. If you are paying with cash, then you are saving the retailer this money. Ask for it to be refunded. If not, then pay with a credit card or take your business elsewhere.

- **Rent or borrow items:** If you rarely use gardening or handyman equipment, why on earth are you buying it? Instead, a better plan is to hire or borrow from friends, family members or neighbours. It will ultimately cost you a lot less.

- **Wait 30 days:** Before making any major purchases, have a rule that you will wait 30 days before making a final decision. During that time, use every opportunity to look for a lower price and try and talk yourself out of the purchase if possible.

- **Sell before you buy**: If you are replacing anything in your home (including your car), have a rule that you must sell the old version before buying anything new. This helps prevent a huge pileup of clutter and forces you to stop and really think about your real needs.

- **Do it Yourself (DIY):** Wherever possible, if you can do the job yourself then give it a go. Look at home improvement videos on YouTube to get an idea of what is possible. This tip works well for simple tasks like lawn-mowing, painting or window cleaning. However, more complicated tasks like plumbing or electrical work should always be done by a professional. Remember the golden rule is to always get three, independent quotes before signing up for any service.

- **Frame photographs**: Instead of spending money on expensive wall prints or paintings, enlarge good family photographs and frame them.

- **Buy a laptop**: When it's time to replace your desktop computer, give careful consideration to buying a portable, second-hand laptop. Why? A laptop can be taken to a library (or work) which means you have very little running costs. Plus, libraries have free heating, cooling, toilets and water.

- **Swap with friends:** If you have items around your home that you are not using such as a spare television set or an unused DVD player, then ask your friends if they have anything to swap in return. You could find that old, dust-gathering television set turns into a fantastic food blender for zero cost and effort.

- **Redecorate with flowers:** It doesn't matter whether the flowers are fresh from the garden or if they are the plastic variety, a vase filled with flowers always brightens a room.

- **Camouflage the lounge:** If your lounge is really old and has stains and tatty cushions, hide the reality with some colourful, cheap throws or cushions. Similarly, if your carpet has seen better days, hide any really obvious marks with rugs or floor mats.

- **Move the furniture:** For an instant lift to your home, simply move the furniture around or get the kids to swap bedrooms. Not only does it give you an opportunity to vacuum and clean areas that are hard to reach, it also creates a fresh feel to your home.

- **Brighten up with paint:** Compared with other redecorating options, paint is one of the cheapest on offer. Use it to create a feature wall or to give new life to old furniture.

- **Add life:** Nothing lifts a room faster than strategically placed pot plants or an aquarium filled with brightly coloured fish.

- **Keep to a theme:** If you have every room a different colour scheme or style of furniture it can make it very difficult to mix and match things as the years go by. It also can make a home feel like a childcare centre. Far better to decide on a central colour scheme and get maximum value for your decorating budget. It also helps when you come to sell your home as neutral, consistent colours are less likely to offend potential buyers.

5.13 Children

It is a well-known fact that raising children can cost a lot of money. Advertising companies are particularly adept at pulling the heart strings to make you think you need to buy their product to be a good parent. One of the best heart string pullers in the business are the disposable nappy (diaper) companies. All those 'comfortable and dry' babies in expensive nappies are such a pretty picture of happiness and contentment. Oh, and 'dry' – remember – these babies are 'dry'. It truly makes you wonder how our ancestors managed to raise children in the days before disposable nappies were invented. However, they did somehow manage to do it and that means you can too!

Cloth nappies are a bit fiddlier and obviously require washing, but the savings are going to be well worth it. Put the money you've saved into something that really matters to your child – like a good education, swimming lessons or orthodontic treatment. Remember to give their little bottoms a good coating of barrier crème and you'll avoid any nasty nappy rash. For those times when you are travelling and cloth nappies won't work, make sure you use store-brand disposable nappies. Besides, they are likely to be made in the same factories making the expensive brand name nappies. Of course, they are not going to have as much padding (which is why they are cheaper), but seriously how much extra 'comfort' is your baby getting? You are going to change a soiled nappy regardless of how long it's been worn! Other areas to save money include:

- **Breast feed**: Quite simply, if you *can* breast feed then try and do it for as long as possible. Unfortunately, for a whole host of reasons, there are women who can't breast feed and they should not have a major guilt trip thrust upon them. Parenthood is a tough enough challenge as it is and everyone needs to learn to support new mothers a lot more. Breast feeding is only one very tiny part of parenthood. However, breast feeding does have lots of benefits for both the mother and the baby and one of the big ones is that it's much cheaper than formula milk. It is also a great way for the mother to lose any additional weight gained during the pregnancy. Plus, there are no dirty bottles to sterilise or re-heat.

- **Buy a blender**: Forget buying all that expensive baby food in jars and packets. Simply throw fruit or vegetables into the blender. The result is a much healthier diet for your baby and a much healthier bank balance for yourself.

- **Buy second hand clothes**: Once you see how fast children grow in their first 2 years of life, you will truly understand why it is insane to buy expensive, trendy clothes for children that only fit them for three months (at best).

- **Sell outgrown clothes:** Many people are given baby clothes that are never worn because they the child outgrows them too quickly. In this case, selling them on eBay (www.ebay.com) to turn unused clothes into cash.

- **Make reusable baby wipes**: Get CHUX cleaning cloths and cut them into smaller squares. Put them into a clean ice-cream container containing a small amount of water and sorbelene cream. Wring them out before using them and then afterwards wash them in the laundry sink so they can be reused.

- **Form a baby-sitting club**: Why pay very expensive child care fees? If you know other mothers who are going back to work part-time, then do a deal where you look after their children if they reciprocate the favour.

- **Join kids' clubs**: When it is free to join, sign your children up as they often have free discount vouchers and other goodies when it's their birthday.

- **Reuse swimming nappies:** Disposable swimming nappies are very expensive so it's important to get maximum use from them. If they have not been soiled, wring them out and dry on the clothes line to be used again.

- **Hire baby items**: For items like bassinets, high chairs and car seats it may make better sense to hire rather than buy these items. However, it does depend on how many children you intend to have as it may actually be worth buying them second hand and then re-selling them after you've used them.

- **Forget the flash bedroom:** Don't waste money buying themed items for your baby's bedroom. They will never know the difference between expensive, brand-name sheets, blankets, cots or strollers. Consider the astronomical expenses ahead of you and cut costs where it doesn't matter.

- **Check government benefits**: Ideally check up on benefits before you have a baby. Once the little one arrives, you may find it hard to concentrate on anything for a few months (if not years – depending on whether you have been blessed with a 'sleeper' or a 'non-sleeper').

- **Determine company benefits:** Most companies offer some form of maternity benefits or parental leave provisions. Find out as soon as possible what options are available from your workplace.

- **Plan the birth date**: Of course, much is in the hands of nature, but you can make significant savings in childcare costs by having a baby that is born close to the cut-off age for school entry. For example, if the school year begins in January and the rule is that all children must be 5 year's old by 30th April in that year, it would be ideal to have a baby born in the January-April period.

  This means the child would need less than 5 years of childcare before entering school. However, a child born in May would need an additional 8 or 9 months of childcare. This adds up to a lot of additional money for parents to pay out in childcare fees!

- **Get them a part-time job**: As soon as your children are old enough, get them working in a part-time job. It gives them independence, responsibility, experience, self-discipline and teaches them the value of money.

- **Skip expensive fads**: In your area, it might be trendy to start children in music classes when they are 6 months old or some other vital baby Einstein-type programme. Resist the pressure as in the first 2-3 years of a baby's life, you can achieve even better results by paying lots of attention to your children, singing songs and reading them **lots** of books (from the library).

- **Postpone large parties**: If you are planning a large party for a child under 5 year's old, then the truth is that you really planning a party for yourself. Kids simply cannot comprehend the difference between 3 and 30 gifts. Plus, most of them won't even remember the event anyway. Save your money and hold a small family-only party for young children. As they get older, review the decision but don't ever go overboard for birthday parties. Remember you still need to get them through high school and tertiary education. Keep site of those major expenses in the future to keep a firm lid on your spending.

Golden Tip: Kiddy consumerism pressures parents to buy the latest toy, pram, clothes etc. Children simply don't need anywhere near as much stuff as our advertising industry tells us. Instead - they need lots of positive attention from both parents. In the end, children will remember your presence far more than the presents you buy them.

6. FRUGAL MEALS

"Breakfast like a king, lunch like a prince and dinner like a pauper."

Before you step into a grocery store, you need to plan out your menu for the week (or fortnight). It's really just common sense that if you fail to put together a menu plan, then you'll end up wasting money and eating a diet that is less than nutritious. Eating a healthier diet is a simple five step process. Unfortunately, too many people skip steps 1, 2 and 4 and buy takeaway foods that are inevitably low in nutrition and high in fat, sugar, salt, calories **and** price!

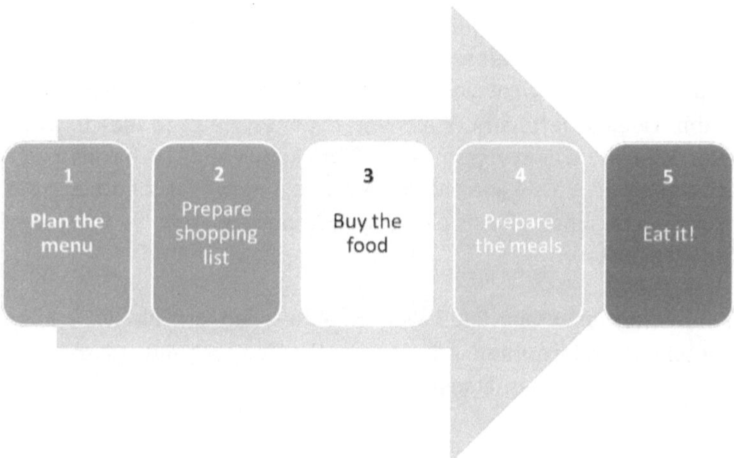

6.1.1 Get Started - Breakfast

To keep things simple, everyone needs to eat a healthy, low-sugar, high fibre cereal for breakfast. It is quick to prepare and one of the cheapest options for breakfast. For a mid-morning snack, always have fruit such as apples, oranges or bananas. This automatically gives you one point in the goal of reaching 'Five a Day' which is something very few people actually achieve! The 'Five a Day' slogan is to remind us that for the ideal diet you should consume five portions of fruit or vegetables each day. If you are going to get anywhere close to achieving this goal – especially for your kids – it's going to take some serious vegetable hiding skills. Of course, it always helps if you start them early on the vegetable and fruit habit so they don't know any differently. Studies have shown that the diet you feed your children in the first seven years of their life sets their eating patterns for the rest of their life. Old childhood habits can be very hard to break for an adult.

6.1.2 Lunch

In this age of obesity, you have maximum chance of burning off what you eat if it is consumed earlier in the day. So, make sure that breakfast and lunch are always bigger meals than dinner.

Lunch should always include a piece of fruit and a serving of calcium such as yoghurt or cheese. What you have next really comes down to personal taste, what you intend eating for dinner and what's left in the fridge as leftovers. However, it's always a good idea to avoid overdoing the wheat / grains and if you know you'll be having pasta for dinner, then it's a good idea to avoid eating wheat (or other types of grains) for lunch. This is particularly important if you've had cereal for breakfast.

Sandwiches or wraps filled with healthy salad are always a good option for children and are yet another opportunity to sneak in further fruit and vegetables!

6.1.3 Dinner

It's dinner time and by now you should be sitting on a minimum score of 2/5 with the goal of sneaking in 3 vegetables into your evening meal. How hard can it be? Remember also that you should only eat meat (of any kind) every other day. So, it's one day with meat, the next day without, one day with meat, the next day without etc. Listed in the following section are seven easy recipes that will easily feed a family of four with leftovers for lunch the following day.

6.1.4 Healthy Eating Pyramid

The famous food pyramid shown below gives a guide to the foods we need to eat most and those which we should eat least. People need to eat more fruit and vegetables in their diet. Foods which are high in sugar and fat need to be limited because they typically lack nutritional value and are effectively wasted calories or kilojoules. Remember also that drinks can be very high in kilojoules and can be the downfall of many people trying to lose weight. Aim to minimise the amount of alcohol, tea, coffee, carbonated drinks (soda) and juices. Try to maximise the amount of water you drink to not only improve your health but your bank balance! The goal should be at least 1 litre of water each day.

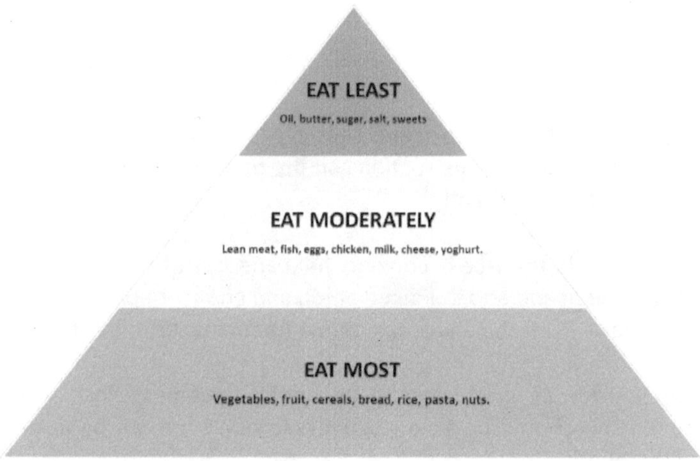

1. Tuna Mornay

Rice (2 cups)
2 tablespoons (50g) of butter (or margarine)
1 tin canned corn – drained
1 medium brown onion – diced
1 large can of tuna (in spring water or brine) – drained
¼ cup (50g) plain flour
2 cups (500ml) of milk
3 tablespoons Dijon mustard or pinch of paprika
1 cup of grated cheese (optional)
1/2 cup frozen peas (optional)
Chopped parsley - sprinkle (optional)
Salt & pepper – sprinkle (optional)

Serves four adults.

Step 1: Cook the rice, corn and peas in a large saucepan of boiling water and follow the instructions on the packet as the time varies depending on the brand.

Step 2: While the rice is cooking, heat the butter in a frypan on medium heat and add the diced onion and cook for approximately 5 minutes. Turn the saucepan to low heat and stir in the flour.

Step 3: Add milk gradually and stir until it becomes a thick white sauce. This should be a slow process so don't hurry it by turning up the heat!

Step 4: Add the cheese and stir into the sauce mix with the mustard / paprika until it is completed melted.

Step 5: Add the tuna and a sprinkle of salt/pepper to the saucepan. Cook on low heat for approximately 10 minutes.

Step 6: Drain the rice and rinse under hot water.

Step 7: Divide the rice into portions. Spoon the tuna mornay over the top of each bowl. Sprinkle with cheese & parsley if desired.

3 Rabbit Food

4 large leaves of iceberg lettuce
4 tomatoes - sliced
3 carrots – grated
Tin beetroot – drained
Tin corn – drained
1 cup grated cheese
1 capsicum – sliced
1 cup frozen peas
4 potatoes
1 small packet of sultanas (50g)
200g broccoli or cauliflower
Any other vegetable in season.
Salt / Pepper

Serves four adults.

Step 1: Place all cut vegetables (corn, peas, potatoes, broccoli, cauliflower) into a microwave container with water and cook until tender.

Step 2: Mix grated carrot, grated cheese, sliced capsicum and sultanas in a large bowl.

Step 3: Divide the lettuce, tomatoes, mixed carrot, cheese, capsicum and sultanas between 4 large bowls. Add steamed vegetables as desired. Sprinkle additional cheese onto vegetables. Add salt & pepper to taste. Enjoy!

4 Apricot Chicken

Rice (2 cups)
1kg skinless chicken breasts
1 tin canned corn – drained
1 medium brown onion – sliced
450g can of apricot nectar (or as close to this size as available)
10 dried apricot pieces
1 packet of French onion soup
½ cup plain flour
1 cup frozen peas (optional)

Serves four adults.

Step 1: Pre-heat the oven to 200 degrees Celsius.

Step 2: Cook the rice, corn and peas in a large saucepan of boiling water and follow the instructions on the packet as the time varies depending on the brand.

Step 3: While the rice is cooking, coat the chicken in flour and place in a casserole dish.

Step 4: In a jug, mix the apricot nectar and French onion soup.

Step 5: Pour the mix over the chicken. Add apricot pieces and cook in the oven for 1 hour. Make sure the casserole dish is covered with its lid.

Step 6: Drain the rice and rinse under hot water.

Step 7: Divide the rice into portions for each person. Give each person at least one piece of chicken. Spoon apricot sauce generously.

6. Cheesy Potato Bake

1kg potatoes unpeeled and chopped into quarters.
2 tablespoons (50g) of butter (or margarine)
1 onion, finely chopped
2 cups (500ml) milk
¼ cup plain flour
2 cups grated cheese
1 carrot – grated (optional)
1 tin of corn (optional)

Serves four adults.

Step 1: Pre-heat the oven to 200 degrees Celsius.

Step 2: Place potatoes in a saucepan. Cover with water and add pinch salt. Boil until potatoes are cooked.

Step 3: Heat the butter in a saucepan on low heat and stir in the flour.

Step 4: Add milk gradually and stir until it becomes a thick white sauce. This is not a fast process so don't hurry it!

Step 5: Add grated carrot, corn, diced onion and 1 cup of cheese to sauce mix and stir until combined well.

Step 6: Grease a large square baking dish or line with baking paper.

Step 7: Place ½ of the potatoes in the baking dish and cover with white cheese sauce mix. Then place the remaining potatoes on top again and cover with the rest of the white cheese sauce mix. Sprinkle the top with remaining cheese.

Step 8: Bake in oven for 20 minutes.

7. Spaghetti Bolognaise

400g spaghetti
400g lamb (or beef) mince
1 tablespoon olive (or vegetable) oil
400g jar tomato pasta sauce
1 medium brown onion – diced
1 carrot – grated (optional)
1 capsicum – sliced finely (optional)

Serves four adults

Step 1: Cook the spaghetti in a saucepan of boiling water and follow the instructions on the packet as the time varies for each brand. When cooked drain the spaghetti and wash under hot water.

Step 2: While the spaghetti is cooking, heat the oil in a fry pan on medium heat and add the diced onion, carrot and capsicum to cook for 5 minutes. Add mince and cook for approximately 6-8 minutes until browned. Use a wooden spoon to break up the mince into smaller pieces. You will know when the mince is cooked as it will no longer be pink.

Step 3: Add the jar of tomato pasta sauce to the fry pan and cook the mince with the sauce (on low heat) for a further 10 minutes or until the sauce is warm/hot.

Step 4: Divide the pasta into portions for each person. Spoon the mince with sauce over the top of the spaghetti.

7. DISASTER PLAN

"It wasn't raining when Noah built the ark" – Howard Ruff

7.1 Introduction

In large offices and government departments, it *always* starts with the pot plants. If you see all those lovely green, healthy plants being lined up in a removal truck, you have been warned. Another key sign is the sudden appearance of external business consultants hired by your company. They are as good a sign (if not better) than the pot plants. Consultants are a popular choice for companies that are looking to cut costs by sacking staff. Of course, nobody in management ever says that consultants are being brought in to perform this task. Instead, they are being brought in to 'increase efficiency' or 'install a new IT system'. Rest assured, consultants always have staff redundancies in mind - even if it's just to take your job. Management especially love them when they recommend staff cuts because it distances them from doing the dirty work themselves.

Other signs of impending doom are board members or senior staff suddenly leaving to pursue new opportunities or selling off large amounts of company shares or options. Also watch out for things like: announcements signalling a company restructure, lots of closed-door meetings, cancelled projects, bad press, low morale, hiring freezes or staff benefits being cut or phased out.

Soon after these telling signs, the rumours usually start and they spread like wild fire. Somebody heard something about 'sales being down'. Another person heard about 'voluntary redundancies'. The rumours then gather pace and are only limited by people's imagination. Naturally management catches wind and holds a meeting designed to reassure people that everything is going along just fine (or words to that effect). This meeting is to try and stop 'good people' from heading to the exits as fast as they can. However, it's really the equivalent of an activated fire alarm for your career and a final warning to start enacting your personal Disaster Plan as fast as you can.

But how do you prepare a plan? Where do you start? This section details the steps to follow if you want to be ready to hit the ground running <u>before</u> you get tapped on the shoulder.

Remember, if you plan to panic then do it early. Never bother to attend a performance review if you know that security guards will be in attendance. Just pack your bags, set your email account out of office notification to 'unavailable' and leave the building quickly! Many companies are concerned about staff becoming violent and damaging equipment when they leave. To prevent this happening, they often escort terminated employees from the building. Avoid the indignity and make sure your personal possessions at work are as few as possible. If ever there was a time to be unwell then this is it. Remember you **are** genuinely sick – sick with worry!

7.2 Pre-Planning

If you think that redundancy or bankruptcy is just around the corner, follow these steps to prepare yourself in advance. The more prepared you are for disaster, the better your chances of survival.

- **Make a budget**: Start by creating a list of essential monthly bills. Remember that essential items do not include things like gym memberships or magazine subscriptions. Instead it means things like rent or mortgage repayments, electricity, gas and food bills. These are the things that if you lost your job, you would still *need* to pay. Start up a second list of everything else you spend your money on that wasn't on the essential list. Notice which list is longer? Usually it's the non-essential items.

- **Sell up quickly**: If you don't have a buffer fund of emergency cash, then you need to get one very, very quickly. Sell what you can and do it as fast as possible. Pawn shops or cash converters can give you quick money for things that you no longer need.

- **Redundancy policy:** Using discretion, find out if you are entitled to anything from your employer if they terminate your job. If there is a call for redundancies, then do your maths as it might be best to get some benefit rather than wait until it goes into liquidation – and you get nothing!

- **Make use of entitlements:** Get as much training or other job entitlements as possible before you walk out the door. If there is a possibility that you will not get paid out your annual leave because the company is going broke, arrange to take a holiday as quickly as possible. Bankrupt companies are very unlikely to make provision for these trivial types of things when winding things up!

- **Update your resume**: Start checking out the market for other employers in your industry. This is all part of being prepared and ensuring you can hit the ground running if the worst-case scenario eventuates. Keep your resume simple and highlight your achievements.

- **Register with recruitment agents**: Depending on your job classification, start talking with job agencies and putting your feelers out for other opportunities in the market place.

- **Apply for jobs**: The best time to apply for another job is while you are still in one. If you suspect that your job will be made redundant then you are probably right. Besides, going to interviews gives you practice for the main event when you really need a job. So, get your name out in the market and start job hunting early before everyone else in your field is doing the same thing. If your kids are old enough to work, then get them into after-school jobs as well. Every dollar helps!

- **Talk to friends and family**: Be open with people about your situation. Don't try to hide the possibility (or reality) of unemployment. Start networking and let everyone know you are looking for work.

- **Outperform in your job**: Now is the time to come forth with great cost-cutting ideas for your company. If you've been storing up your creative, innovative ideas for a long time, now is the time to show off your brilliance and outperform your fellow worker.

- **Government benefits**: A quick phone call to the relevant government department will give you the information on social security benefits that may be available if you lose your job.

Knowing how much you could get will help you determine if more dramatic cost-cutting is required.

- **Clear your desk:** If you are made redundant, a quick clean of your desk makes for a fast getaway.

7.3 Redundancy

"In the middle of difficulty lies opportunity." - Albert Einstein

7.3.1 Stages of Grief

Redundancy is a very distressing and traumatic time for most people. Recognise that your stress levels are going to be tested and try to take things one step at a time. Making rash decisions that come back to bite you later will only make things worse. This is when all the preparation you have done in the past will pay handsome dividends by helping you focus on the tasks that lie ahead. This gets you ahead of the game because all your co-workers who have also been made redundant will be running around in a blind panic not knowing what to do. If by some chance they did manage to keep their jobs, rest assured they are also experiencing the stress of knowing that one (or all) of them will be next.

Like any loss in life, the process of redundancy involves various stages of grieving. How deep and long each stage lasts depends on your personal situation. For example, someone who has six children to support on one income and has limited chance of finding a new job is going to have a very different experience to someone who is close to retirement and has a strong buffer of cash. Grief is also a complex emotion because often someone who has reached the point of acceptance can easily slip back into anger or denial and the cycle repeats itself. Here is a brief explanation of the stages:

1. **Shock**: This is the big moment when you've been told that your job no longer exists. The writing could have been on the wall for ages, but when the axe finally falls it is still just as painful. The most important thing to remember is to avoid saying or doing anything as it could easily end up being your biggest regret. KEEP CALM. If possible, remove the temptation to say what you really think and get yourself home immediately. Just say that you are sick. Don't stress for one millisecond about the truth of the matter as nobody will really care anyway.

2. **Denial:** Finally, you are home and have either been told not to come into work anymore or you have been given an 'end date' to finish up your job. This is when the entire situation may well feel like a bad dream or a nightmare. Denial is the way nature protects your mind from information overload. The only cure for this stage is time and most people are over this phase in around 24 - 48 hours.

3. **Anger**: This is the hardest phase of the entire process and also the most dangerous one. It's the moment when you realise that you are the one taking the punishment for management's incompetence while they hold onto their comfortable lifestyle. It's also the time where you question, "Why me? Why not someone else?" It's hard. It's very, very hard to get through this phase straight up. However, the faster you get through this stage, the faster your chances of rebuilding your life. Channel your anger into positive pursuits by running, swimming, punching a pillow or whatever else works to release the anger. Remember to avoid alcohol or illegal activities as it will only make things worse.

4. **Acceptance**: At last you have worked through the shock, denial and anger and are ready to start rebuilding your career. You've moved on from the past and are now focussing on the future. The emotional tornado of the previous few weeks or months is subsiding and you can finally start thinking creatively about your future options.

5. **Recovery**: This is the stage where you are actively looking for work either with another company or have made the decision to start your own business. Don't rule out the option of doing both! Financial planners always tell clients to never have all their investments (eggs) in the one basket, so neither should you when it comes to income sources. Set simple realistic targets to keep moving forward and remember to keep active and focussed on the task ahead.

7.3.2 What to Do

To hit the ground running, follow these 13 tips in the recovery stage:

- **Negotiate:** Never, ever, ever accept the first offer a company makes to you with regard to a payout. With a little imagination, you can do better. Ask for additional benefits such as an extended period of health or life insurance, outplacement services, additional car lease benefits or even gardening leave where they continue to pay you throughout your notice period but you are not required to be in the office. Don't close the door on the possibility of returning to the company at a later date, so always speak positively of your work and colleagues. If you can't manage to do that, then say nothing!

- **Avoid exit interviews**: There is absolutely nothing for you to gain by attending one of these meetings. In fact, you have everything to lose from the experience as you will be sorely tempted to tell the company exactly how things are in their god-forsaken fertiliser heap of a company. Save yourself the future regret and gracefully decline the invitation. Unless of course, you are in a positive frame of mind and think you can use the opportunity to push yourself to the top of the short-list when the company starts to re-hire again.

- **Gather references**: Another important reason not to go all out telling the company what you really think of their redundancy process is because you will require references in the future. You may have worked solidly for the last 5 or 10 years but if you go out on bad terms then everything good will be forgotten in the blink of an eye.

- **Register for unemployment benefits:** The sooner your application is received by social security, the faster your benefits can be paid out. Make this one of your first phone calls. Even if you don't qualify, you may still be eligible for other types of benefits.

- **Develop an action mentality**: Successful people have one key trait in common. They *do* things and don't spend time sitting around whinging and complaining about how hard things are for them. Channel all your energy from anger and resentment into finding a new job.

- **Speak to the union:** If your job has union representation, then make use of all those union fees you have contributed to get them to push management for a better severance package.

- **Get professional advice:** If you are due a significant payout then don't go off and blow the money on a new car or holiday. Seek out a financial planner or accountant that can help you make the most of any redundancy payout.

- **Fight depression:** Get outside and exercise at least once a day as this is one of the biggest weapons in the fight against the dark side. Start or keep up with your social network as other people are going to be your best source of support during these challenging times.

- **Review your skills:** Consider the option of reskilling for a new career or up skilling to enhance your job prospects. However, make sure that any further training you do has a high likelihood of improving your employability. If possible, get the government or your former employer to pay the tuition fees as part of your redundancy package.

- **Prepare for interviews:** This means practising answering all sorts of questions about your previous employment, future goals or even old chestnuts like 'What are your key weaknesses?' As if you are really going to tell them the horrible truth! Instead, you need to have answers prepared that will roll off the top of your tongue yet seem natural and unforced. It's all part of the game and is a skill that needs to be practised.

- **Plan your ideal job:** Sit down and write up a list of what you liked about your old job and what you hated. Picture the kind of work that you would like to get in the future and imagine or daydream yourself in this role. Don't discount the power of positive visualisation. If you can dream it then you have a much greater chance of achieving it in the future. Set clear, written goals for the role you want and be as specific as possible.

- **Keep to a routine:** It's all too easy to sink into a routine of watching television or over-eating while waiting for the phone to ring. At first not going into work will feel like a holiday. Then as the weeks go by, it will feel like an extended holiday. Unfortunately, soon after that (around 8 weeks), reality will hit hard and self-esteem issues and depression can quickly set in. Your goal is to stop this happening by establishing a positive routine from the moment you walk out the door of your previous job. Set aside time each day for job searching, skill enhancement, exercising, chores and leisure activities.

- **Talk to your bank:** If you have a mortgage or other debts, examine the possibility of taking a repayment holiday until you find another job. Keep your bank informed of your situation because if you do fall behind in repayments and they have no prior warning then they will be forced to start the foreclosure process.

- **Make lemonade:** When life throws you a lemon, use all the creativity and resourcefulness you can muster by turning it into lemonade. Twist a negative into a positive. Everyone has a mental list of things they would like to do but never had the time. Don't end up looking back on a period of unemployment and regretting how much time was wasted. Remember that all of us only get a certain number of days on this Earth and then it's over. Once you've spent a good couple of hours working at finding a job, take a break and spend time with your family and friends. You'll never, ever regret getting to know them better.

8. MAKING MONEY

"When the going gets tough, the tough get going." - Joseph Kennedy.

Finding a job during a recession is really hard work. The journey can be similar to a roller coaster ride alternating between troughs of depression and peaks of hope and exhilaration. Throw in the financial commitments of a mortgage plus the additional stress of raising children and it can lead to breaking point. Your goal in life is to keep as far away as possible from that point and prepare in advance by establishing an emergency stash of funds in a bank account. If you reach breaking point it can lead to horrible things like divorce, suicide, crime, mental illness etc. It's frightening how quickly things can go from bad to worse when money is involved. Even if you think your job is safe, it's always a good idea to have multiple sources of income as an ongoing backup plan. Here are 23 ways to make money quickly:

- **Enter competitions**: If it is free to enter, then you have nothing to lose and everything to gain by throwing your hat into the ring to win a prize.

- **Complete online surveys:** Again, as long as it's free <u>and</u> you have the time available then make the most of it by completing online surveys for cash! Just be careful to check the terms and conditions to make sure it really is worthwhile.

- **Pose for art classes:** Be warned that this may involve removing your clothes, but it can be a lucrative way to make extra cash.

- **Volunteer for medical trials:** Depending on what the drug company is testing; this can be anything from pocket money to thousands. Just remember to weight up the risks against the benefits.

- **Donate body fluids or hair**: In some countries, including the USA, people get paid for donating blood, plasma (from blood), breast milk, hair, semen or eggs.

- **Create media content**: Sell images and videos online via websites such as: YouTube, Paya, Shutterstock or Gumroad.

- **Start a blog**: Find a topic that you are passionate about and link in with Amazon Affiliates (or other affiliate programmes) for additional income. Start off with a free website such as WordPress, Wix or Blogger.

- **Shelf filling:** This is a tried and tested job that is popular with students as the work is usually done late in the evening or early morning when there are few (if any) customers in the store. This means it's very easy to fit in around lectures or other part-time work.

- **Weekend markets**: Turn a hobby such as sewing, craft, knitting, gardening, cooking or photography into a second source of income by holding a weekend stall at the markets. Goods can also be sold on websites such as Etsy.

- **Taxi driving**: Obviously you will need a license and a police check, but working as a taxi (or cab) driver can be a quick means of getting food on the table.

- **Tutor students**: If you have completed university or college then your skills will be in demand from high school students needing additional help in their studies.

- **Night cleaning**: This is a job that is both easy to learn and get hired quickly. After all, somebody has to keep all those shiny, high-rise office buildings clean. Hospitals, schools, shopping centres and nursing homes are always on the lookout for reliable staff.

- **Call centres**: This type of work is generally easy to get but very stressful to keep doing for long periods of time, particularly if cold-calling is required. However, it is an industry that has a high turnover and work is usually easy to obtain.

- **Childcare:** Many families are crippled by the rising cost of childcare. One solution could be to check out the government regulations for offering family day care. Alternatively, babysit or look after primary school children during the after-school period or holidays.

- **Car advertisements**: In the UK, they have "Uni Car Ads" (www.unicarads.co.uk) where students are paid around 60 pounds a month to place large advertisements on the doors of their cars. In Australia, there is Signrider (www.signrider.com.au) where drivers can get paid around $15 to $80 per week for a similar opportunity. In tough times, this idea can help pay the grocery bills!

- **Be an extra in commercials or movies**: The reality is that very few people have film-star looks or acting ability. However, commercials and movies are always on the lookout for people with ordinary looks to appear in the background going about their daily business.

- **Garden maintenance**: There are plenty of people that don't have the time (or energy) to mow their lawn, rake leaves or weed garden beds. Create a simple paper advertisement and walk the neighbourhood putting them into mailboxes. Place a flyer in the local shop window advertising your services.

- **Part-time jobs**: Fast food outlets are one of the most popular part-time jobs on offer. Don't forget to look at options such as: bartending, taxi driving, pizza delivery, busking, fruit picking, pamphlet distribution, dog walking, temping (secretarial), golf caddie, window cleaning, pool lifeguard or pet sitting.

- **Market research**: Hunt down market research companies in your area and ask to be added to their database. You may find yourself doing all sorts of crazy things like taste-testing cereals or giving feedback on television commercials. Check out websites such as YouData, Survey Savvy and American Consumer Opinion.

- **Mystery shopping**: A close cousin of market research is the often-lucrative job of mystery shopping. The benefits are also known to include free meals or clothing. All you have to do is act like a normal person using a company's services and then complete a survey report afterwards.

- **Translating or interpreting**: Many people speak a second or third language but are oblivious to the potential for creating an income from offering a translation or interpreting service. Use your language skills for tutoring students or teaching in a college or university.

- **Find lost money:** Hunt down lost bank accounts, share dividends, pension or superannuation accounts that have been forgotten. They could be just the miracle lifesaver you have been praying for!!

Country	**Website(s)** ***Remember to check the internet for even more websites.***
Australia	www.moneysmart.gov.au/tools-and-resources/find-unclaimed-money www.ato.gov.au/forms/searching-for-lost-super/
New Zealand	www.treasury.govt.nz/abouttreasury/services/unclaimedmoney
United Kingdom	Unclaimedassets.co.uk
USA	www.unclaimedassets.com www.usa.gov/unclaimed-money

- **Home care services**: Nearly all western countries have ageing populations and many elderly people are reluctant to move into nursing homes or retirement villages as they want to stay in their own homes as long as possible. This means there is an ever-increasing demand for home care staff. Either sign up with a recruitment agency or advertise locally by placing an advertisement in the papers.

- **Rent a room:** If you have a spare room, rent it out to a student. Alternatively, rent out your garage as additional storage or driveway as parking. However, check out your home insurance policy first.

9. USEFUL WEBSITES

9.1.1 Meal Planning

#	Website
1	www.120dollarfoodchallenge.com
2	www.taste.com.au
3	www.bestrecipes.com.au
4	www.jamieoliver.com
5	www.juliegoodwin.com.au
6	www.nigella.com
7	www.allrecipes.com

9.1.2 Home Living

#	Website
1	organizedhome.com
2	www.marthastewart.com
3	www.goodhousekeeping.com
4	www.realsimple.com
5	www.midwaysimplicity.com
6	www.becomingminimalist.com

9.1.3 Frugal Living

#	Website
1	www.simplesavings.com.au
2	www.zenhabits.net
3	www.wisebread.com
4	www.livingonadime.com
5	www.frugalandthriving.com.au
6	www.thrifty-living.org.uk

9.1.4 Saving Money

#	Website
1	www.moneysmart.gov.au
2	www.kidspot.com.au
3	www.savingsguide.com.au
4	www.moneysavingexpert.com
5	www.mymoney.gov
6	www.thisismoney.co.uk
7	www.moneyadviceservice.co.uk
9	www.savingsguide.com.au

10. ESSENTIAL READING & VIDEOS

"The man who does not read has no advantage over the man who cannot read." - Mark Twain

10.1 Books

#	Title	Author
1	The Complete Tightwad Gazette	Amy Dacyczyn
2	Rich Dad, Poor Dad	Robert Kiyosaki
3	A Gift to my Children: A Father's Lessons for Life & Investing	Jim Rogers
4	Organizing for Life: Declutter your Mind to Declutter your World	Sandra Felton
5	The Joy of Less – A Minimalist Living Guide	Francine Jay
6	Money Made Simple: How to Flawlessly Control Your Finances in Minutes a Year	Stacy Johnson
7	Your Money or Your Life: Transforming Your Relationship with Money and Achieving Financial Independence	Vicki Robin
8	The Richest Man in Babylon	George Clason

REMEMBER: Try to borrow these books from the library or a friend.

10.2 YouTube Videos

#	Title	Time
1	Randy Pausch's Last Lecture: Achieving Your Dreams	1:16:27
2	Music and Life – Alan Watts	2:22
3	Commencement Address – Steve Jobs	14:34
4	Peter Walsh: The Clutter Buster	2:18
5	Economic Collapse – How the Banks Won	44:26

Go to www.youtube.com and type in the titles listed above to view these videos.

www.ingramcontent.com/pod-product-compliance
Lightning Source LLC
LaVergne TN
LVHW100317210926
848480LV00003B/1156